INSIGHT COMPACT GUIDES

Peak DISTRICT

Compact Guide: Peak District is the ideal quick-reference guide to this delightful and varied region. It tells you all you need to know about the Peak's attractions, from bracing gritstone edges to intimate limestone dales and fine stately homes to fascinating museums and customs.

This is one of more than 70 titles in *Apa Publications'* new series of pocket-sized, easy-to-use guidebooks intended for the independent-minded traveller. *Compact Guides* are in essence travel encyclopedias in miniature, designed to be comprehensive yet portable, as well as up-to-date and authoritative.

Star Attractions

An instant reference to some of the Peak District's top attractions to help you on your way.

Old Glossop p17

Macclesfield silk p20

Buxton Opera p27

Buxton Pavilion Gardens p28

Bakewell puddings p50

Stanage Edge p32

Derwent Dams p38

Castleton p39

Treak Cliff Cavern p41

Tideswell Church p45

Dovedale p59

Peak DISTRICT

Introduction

Places

Culture

Leisure

Practical Information

Peak District – The Best of Both Worlds

Opposite: abseiling off Stanage Edge

The Peak District is misleadingly named. Visitors seek in vain for the sharply-pointed mountain tops that might be expected from the usual dictionary definition of 'peak'. In fact, the name comes from the Old English *peac*, which simply meant a hill. The first recorded mention is in the late 7th-century *Tribal Hidage*, which refers to a tribe called the Pecsaetan – the dwellers of the Peak. In the 10th-century *Anglo Saxon Chronicle*, the area was known as Peacclond – the hilly land.

The Peak District stands at the crossroads of Britain. Situated in the very heart of the country, it marks both the end of the lowlands and the start of the uplands. This unique position gives the hills and dales of the Peak the best of both worlds – and an intriguing combination of flora and fauna. Lying at the southern extremity of the Pennines, the Peak District is the last knobbly vertebrae in what used to be called 'the backbone of England'. It represents the first real hill country for travellers heading north from London and the southeast.

The Peak has often been described as an inland island, a fact which is most evident when travelling at night across the bleak moors of the west or east of the district. From this dark vantage point, the street lights of the surrounding cities on the plain below spread out in a sparkling reef of orange neon. Half the population of England lives within 60 miles of its centre, and from the northern conurbations come most of the estimated 22-million visitors to the Peak District National Park. For many generations of mill and factory workers in the cities of Manchester and Sheffield on either side, the Peak has represented freedom from the drudge of their everyday lives. Ewan MacColl's classic walker's anthem, *The Manchester Rambler*, expresses it perfectly:

> *I may be a wage slave on Monday*
> *But I am a free man on Sunday*

Those Manchester ramblers come to enjoy an unparalleled range of landscapes and walking opportunities a cheap bus or train ride away from their homes. To the north, west and east of the compact, 600-sq mile (1,550-sq km) area, they can wander freely on the high, millstone grit moors, which reach over 2,000ft (600m) on the peaty plateaus of Kinder Scout (high point 2,088ft/636m) and Bleaklow. Alternatively, they can enjoy the gentler pleasures of strolling across the broad 1,000-ft (300-m) limestone plateau in the centre and south of the Peak, which is dissected by steep-sided, craggy dales, the most famous of which are Dove Dale, Monsal Dale and Lathkill Dale.

Pastoral landscape near Buxton

Remnants of industry past

5

Freedom

Twin Peaks

The two distinct and contrasting landscapes of the grit-stone and the limestone have been given the descriptive names of the Dark and White Peaks. These terms reflect the predominant colour of the underlying rocks and mirror the fabric of the Peak District landscape well.

Exposed rocks on Hallam Moor

Most of the exposed rocks in the Peak District date from the Carboniferous period of 330 million years ago. At that time, the land now known as the Peak District lay under a warm, shallow sea just north of the equator. Millions of tiny sea creatures and corals lived and died in the semi-tropical conditions. And as they died, their microscopic, lime-rich skeletons floated down to the bottom of that shallow sea, building up over the aeons into a massive bed of limestone several thousands of feet deep. The fossils of some of these long-dead sea creatures, the screw-like crinoids (sea-lilies) for instance, can still be seen in dry-stone walls. Some of the limestones, generally those on the edges of the tropical reefs, were harder and more resistant to erosion. They later formed the few peaks in the Peak District, such as Thorpe Cloud and Chrome and Park-house Hills by the River Dove.

Later in the same geological period, vast rivers brought sediments down from fast-eroding mountains in the north and deposited them into the same sea in huge spreading deltas. It was this coarse-grained sediment that eventually formed the hard, abrasive rock known as millstone grit, usually shortened to gritstone, on top of the limestone. At various periods in between, smoother sandy sediments were deposited, forming the shale valleys in which the major rivers of the Wye and Derwent run today.

A landscape formed by ice and fire

Conditions were not always as peaceful as this cycle of sedimentary deposition might indicate. There were sudden, violent interludes, when the timeless process of accretion was disturbed by volcanic activity. This is evidenced by the appearance of dark, basaltic outcrops, known as toadstones, and in some places, hexagonal pillars exposed in quarries like those on Calton Hill or in Tideswell Dale. The sandwich of sedimentary Carboniferous rocks was later uplifted into what is known as the Derbyshire Dome, exposing the limestone at the centre and the gritstone on either side and to the north, creating the distinctive Peak District landform of the 'edges'.

The final polish to the Peak District landscape was added by the immense grinding force of ice age glaciers, which in geological terms finished their work recently – just 10,000 years ago. The broad shallow valleys of the Wye and the Derwent, now graced by the parklands of Chatsworth and Haddon, have been chiselled by glaciers.

The Wye at Bakewell

It was as a direct result of the dying glaciers that the famous Peak District dales were formed. As the last of the gigantic ice rivers melted towards the north, enormous cataracts of abrasive meltwater flooded south and east, carving out the narrow, steep-sided dales that are today the walkers' paradise. Unlike the more spacious Yorkshire Dales and the dales of the northern Pennines, which are usually threaded by roads, the Peak District's more intimate dales are hemmed in by steep crags and caves and can only be visited on foot.

At the crossroads

The limestone dales are the wildlife showplaces of the Peak District. In their secluded defiles, many nationally rare species of flora and fauna find their home at the crossroads between the highland and lowland zones of Britain.

This richness has been officially recognised, and many of the major dales are now protected as part of the Derbyshire Dales National Nature Reserve. Several more are protected as local nature reserves.

Approach with care

The much praised Dove Dale

Rivers like the Dove and Lathkill are among the purest in the country, running for almost their entire length over limestone. This means they support a rich and varied waterlife, including the rare small freshwater lobster known as the crayfish, or locally as a 'crawkie', which can survive only in the cleanest rivers and streams.

The richness of the aquatic life of the limestone rivers was the attraction for one of the first popularisers of the Peak District, Izaak Walton. His book *The Compleat Angler*, first published in 1653, praised Dove Dale as 'the princess of rivers' and 'the finest…that ever I saw and the fullest of fish'. His eulogies were matched by his friend and co-author Charles Cotton of Beresford Hall, who described the Lathkill as 'by many degrees, the purest and most transparent stream that I ever saw, either at home

7

or abroad'. And it bred, he said, 'the reddest and the best Trouts in England'. Those brown and rainbow trout are still there, awaiting the angler's lure in the Dove and Lathkill rivers, but such fine fishing comes pretty expensive these days, and a licence is required to enjoy the sport which they provide.

Free of charge, however, is the abundant bird and animal life of the dales, and the observant visitor can enjoy the iridescent flash of the diving kingfisher, the cutely-curtseying white-bibbed dipper, and the sulphur-yellow and falsely-named grey wagtail bobbing on their banks. Commoner species such as moorhen, coot and mallard are abundant.

Sheep in the heather

The ashwoods are home to the rare, pink-flowered shrub mezereon and white drifts of wood anemones, dog's mercury and ransoms in early summer. The paths through the wooded parts of the dales are decorated with meadowsweet, meadow and bloody cranesbill, red and white campion and tall yellow spikes of mullein.

Flowering meadow

Out on the open, closely-grazed upper parts of the dales, a close mat of herb-rich species covers the ground. Sweet-smelling thyme, yellow rockrose and the red and yellow flowers of bird's foot trefoil ('bacon and eggs') carpet the ground, attracting butterflies like the northern brown argus, meadow brown, green-veined white and small tortoiseshell. Over 50 plant species have been recorded in a square metre of the pastures of Upper Lathkill Dale.

Common mammals such as the fox and badger hunt on these open pastures from their dens either high in the dale or deep in the woods, while overhead, kestrels hover in the wind watching for any movement beneath.

Miniature dales – some of them local nature reserves – were created when the National Park converted disused railway tracks into pleasant, traffic-free, walking and riding routes. Both the Tissington Trail and the High Peak Trail were created this way.

The White Peak plateau above the dales is comparatively sparse in wildlife interest, as modern farming has sprayed out of existence many of the herb-rich hay meadows which used to add so much colour to the stone-walled fields. But there are still significant colonies of lapwing and curlew, and the spiralling song of the skylark brightens the summer scene in this tamed and settled landscape.

Miller's Dale Forest

The only semi-natural woodlands in the Dark Peak (gritstone) area are the isolated pockets of sessile oaks found in rocky cloughs (valleys) like Padley Gorge and above the Ladybower Reservoir on the A57. Here, rare summer visitors such as pied wagtails and redstarts are found. This natural tree cover has been replaced in most of the Dark Peak valleys by serried ranks of alien conifers, planted around the 50 or so reservoirs that have flooded so many dales. The largest are the Upper Derwent reservoirs of Ladybower, Derwent and Howden, built between the wars to supply the East Midlands towns of Nottingham, Leicester and Derby. Others, such as the Longdendale and Goyt Valley reservoirs, supply Manchester and Stockport.

Despite their reputation as wildlife deserts, some of these plantations have been colonised by rare raptors such as the goshawk, while mergansers and common sandpipers use the deep, acid waters of the reservoirs.

Upper Derwent Reservoir

The Dark Peak moors may appear also at first sight to be barren wilderness. Apart from the staccato call of the red grouse, the bird for which many thousands of acres of heather moorland are carefully and exclusively managed, there appears to be little to interest the naturalist. But merlin and peregrines quarter the moorland skies, and the elusive blue or mountain hare, re-introduced in the 19th century for shooting, often shows up in its starkly white winter coat on the bleak peat hags and groughs. Other moorland birds include meadow pipits and the 'guardian of the moors', the beautiful golden plover.

Human influence

Every landscape in the Peak District has been affected to a greater or lesser extent by human intervention. As we have seen, even the high gritstone moors are managed for grouse and sheep, and farming remains the single most important industry in the area.

Traditionally the Peak District has supported a dual economy, with farmers, especially in the White Peak area, doubling as lead miners or quarrymen. Although lead mining finished about a century ago, there are still active fluorspar mines, and large limestone quarries create livid scars in the landscape.

This is a major problem for the Peak National Park authority, set up as the first in Britain in 1951 to conserve and enhance the area and provide opportunities for visitors to enjoy and understand it. Quarries such Eldon Hill near Castleton or Topley Pike near Buxton are obvious blots on this protected landscape. But they are still important as local sources of employment, and as Britain's National Parks remain living and working landscapes, this must to be taken into account.

Pastoral landscape and rural crafts

About 38,000 people live in the Peak National Park and 22 million people visit it each year. Tourism has become a vitally important industry, one that rivals the traditional industries of farming and mineral extraction. It is now worth more than £75 million each year to the local economy. The difficult task facing the National Park authority is to try to balance the needs of local people and the pressure of those millions of visitors who make the Peak the busiest national park in Europe.

9

Historical Highlights

10,000–3500BC Mesolithic hunter-gatherers enter the Peak from Europe, and later Neolithic people build the earliest monuments, e.g. Arbor Low and Bull Ring henges, Five Wells, Tadding-ton and Minninglow chambered tombs.

3500–1000BC Bronze Age settlements appear on eastern moors, e.g. Swine Sty, and the first for-tified structures appear on Carl Wark and Mam Tor. Many burial mounds are raised, and Stanton Moor with Nine Ladies Stone Circle becomes an important burial ground and religious site.

1000BC–AD70 Hill forts, e.g. Mam Tor, Fin Cop and Ball Cross, are built in the Iron Age.

AD70–410 The Romans enter the Peak in search of lead ore deposits. Forts are established at Navio near Brough and Melandra near Glos-sop. Buxton, *Aquae Arnemetiae*, is established as a spa based on the local thermal springs.

410 The Romans withdraw, leaving behind a Romano-British culture and farming settlements.

c675 Tribal Hidage makes first reference to *Pec-saetan*, 'the dwellers of the Peak'.

827 Anglo-Saxons conquer Anglian Mercia, which includes the Peak District. The first Saxon preaching crosses are carved and raised at Bakewell, Eyam and Hope.

874 Viking raids culminate in the annexation of Mercia and the founding of Derby.

920 *The Anglo-Saxon Chronicle* records that Edward the Elder has reconquered the Peak and built a fortress at Bakewell, where he receives the fealty of various northern kings, becoming king of the Scots, Northumbrians and Welsh.

1066 The Norman Conquest.

1069–70 William the Conqueror turns his at-tention to his fractious northern lands and, in what becomes known as the Harrying of the North, parts of the Peak are laid waste.

1086 The Domesday Book records that William owns a substantial settlement at Bakewell, where there are two priests and a church. His son owns Castleton: 'in Peak's Arse, Arnbern and Hund-ing held the land of William Peverel's castle'. Much of the Peak is *wasta est*, 'waste; woodland, unpastured, fit for hunting'.

1157 Henry II receives the fealty of Malcolm IV of Scotland at Peveril Castle.

1275 Edward I visits Tideswell while hunting in the Royal Forest of the Peak.

1288 Edward I promulgates lead mining laws in an Inquisition at Ashbourne known as Quo Warranto. These laws are still in force today.

1305 The boundaries of the Royal Forest of the Peak are set, covering about 40 sq miles (100 sq km) in the centre and north of the Peak Dis-trict. The Forest was used for hunting and ad-ministered under strict laws from Peveril Castle.

c1350 Haddon Hall is rebuilt by Sir Richard Vernon on land once owned by William Peverel.

1400–1500 The great rebuilding. The first Chatsworth is built by Bess of Hardwick, and Tu-dor tower houses such as North Lees Hall are built by local landowners.

1570 Mary Queen of Scots is held at Chatsworth.

1612 *Poly-Olbion*, published by Michael Dray-ton, describes the Seven Wonders of the Peak for the first time.

1636 *De Mirabilibus Pecci* (*Wonders of the Peak*) is published by Thomas Hobbes, philoso-pher and tutor to the Cavendish family.

1651 The Battle of Hartington Moor, a minor skirmish in the English Civil War.

1653 *The Compleat Angler*, a guide for fish-ermen to the Dove and Lathkill, is published by Izaak Walton.

1665–6 The Plague comes to Eyam, killing one in four of the population when the village's self-imposed quarantine stops the disease spreading.

1681 *The Wonders of the Peak* , the first popular tourist guide to the Peak, is published.

1687–1707 Chatsworth is rebuilt in its present Palladian style by the 4th Earl of Devonshire.

1688 Plotters led by the 4th Earl of Devonshire plan the Great Rebellion at Revolution House, Whittington, seeking to overthrow James II.

1716 James Brindley, pioneering civil engineer and canal builder, born at Tunstead, Buxton.

1720 The first Enclosure Acts in the Peak result in the large-scale enclosure of open fields and moors and the building of miles of drystone walls.

1742 Silk production begins in Macclesfield.

1758 A well-dressing ceremony at Tissington is the first to be described in written records.

1771 Richard Arkwright builds the first water-powered cotton mill at Cromford, near Matlock, heralding the start of the Industrial Revolution.

1780–4 The 5th Duke of Devonshire builds The Crescent at Buxton, funded by profits from his copper mines at Ecton Hill, Staffordshire.

1796–7 There are riots in Bakewell against the Militia Ballot Act.

1815 At Derbyshire's last public gibbeting, Anthony Lingard is executed at Wardlow Mires.

1830 The Railway Age arrives with the construction of the Cromford and High Peak Railway between the Cromford Canal and Hurdlow, near Buxton. Originally planned as a canal, this pioneering route reached 1,264ft (385m) while crossing the limestone plateau.

1848–77 The Longdendale reservoirs are built to supply water to the expanding industrial city of Manchester. They form the largest man-made expanse of water in the world.

1860 The Midland line is constructed through the Wye Valley, linking Matlock and Manchester and exciting the wrath of John Ruskin.

1899 The failure of the Ashbourne to Buxton line marks the end of the railway building era.

1901–16 The Howden and Derwent reservoirs are built in the Upper Derwent Valley, serving Sheffield and the East Midlands.

1905 The Buxton Opera House is designed by Frank Matcham and built in the Edwardian style.

1932 After a mass Trespass on Kinder Scout five ramblers are imprisoned. Their sentence catalyses movements demanding access to mountains and National Parks.

1935–45 The Ladybower Reservoir fills the Upper Derwent Valley, depopulating and drowning the villages of Derwent and Ashopton.

1949 The National Parks and Access to the Countryside Act is passed.

1951 The Peak District National Park is created, the first of its kind in Britain.

1954 The first rights of access are agreed in the Peak District, and the first National Park Ranger (then Warden) Service is created.

1965 Tom Stephenson's 250-mile (400-km) Pennine Way is opened. It is Britain's first long-distance footpath, linking Edale with Kirk Yetholm just over the Scottish Border.

1967–8 The Tissington and High Peak Trails replace the pulled-up tracks of the Ashbourne to Buxton and Cromford and High Peak railways.

1972 The new Derbyshire Dales National Nature Reserve includes Lathkill Dale, Cressbrook Dale and Monks Dale.

1987 The Festival of National Parks is held at at Chatsworth Park.

1997 A new constitution is written for the Peak District National Park.

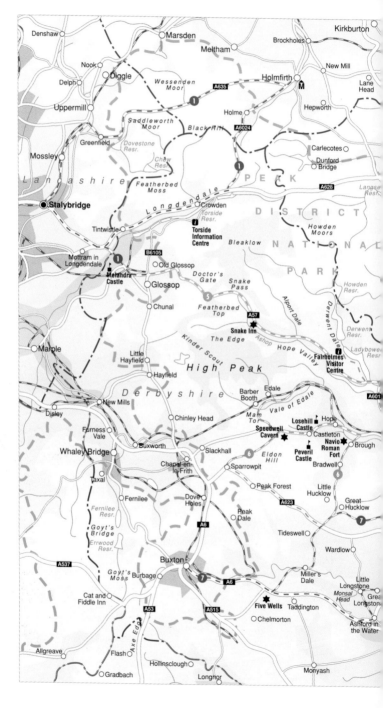

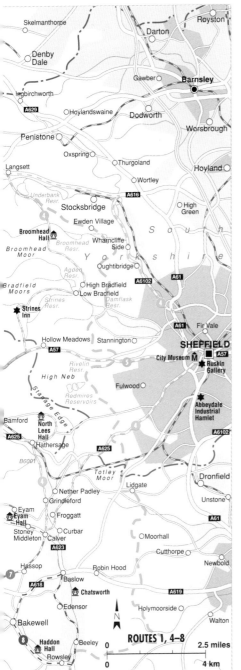

15

Castleton, Route 6
Bakewell, Route 8

Old Glossop, Route 1

ROUTES 1, 4–8

0 — 2.5 miles
0 — 4 km

Practice makes perfect on Holme Moss

Preceding pages: the vast landscape from Stanage

Pre-industrial Old Glossop

Glossop: the central square

Route 1

The Northern Moors and Summer Wine Country

Glossop – Longdendale – Holmfirth – Wessenden Head
– Dove Stone – Stalybridge – Mottram in Longdendale
– Glossop (**40 miles / 65km**) *See map on pages 14–15*

Compared to Bakewell, Matlock and Dove Dale, the far
north of the National Park receives few visitors. It is a high,
wild country of desolate moorland and long valleys, often
flooded by reservoirs constructed to slake the insatiable
thirst of the surrounding cities and towns spawned by the
Industrial Revolution.

For the populations of those conurbations, the moors
are an essential escape for true recreation at the weekends.
These moors bred hardy walkers known with good reason
as 'bogtrotters': some of the most serious – if squelchy
– walking in the area is to be found here.

But on either side of the moors, which are crossed by
trans-Pennine roads often closed by snow in winter, there
are a number of charming gritstone villages. Places like
Holme and Holmfirth have achieved wide fame as loca-
tions for the long-running BBC Television comedy series, *Last of the Summer Wine*. A whole tourist industry
has been built around the exploits of Foggy, Clegg and
Compo in the former mill town of Holmfirth, and many
people come to visit Norah Batty's house and the im-
probably-named Wrinkled Stocking Cafe.

The route starts in the industrial township of **Glossop**,
which owes its spacious and elegant central square and
civic buildings to the early 19th-century patronage of the
11th Duke of Norfolk. Glossop's wealth was founded on

textiles, and at the turn of the 19th century, there were no fewer than 56 mills in the district, mostly processing cotton. The 'industrial quarter' of Glossop is still known as Howardtown, taking the family name of the Lord of the Manor. **★★ Old Glossop** retains the unspoilt air of the pre-industrial village, with a range of charming 17th-century gritstone houses. The story of Glossop and district is well-told in the **★★ Glossop Heritage Centre** in Henry Street, just off Norfolk Square (open all year, Monday to Saturday 10.30am–4.30pm), which also has regular exhibitions by local artists.

Earlier settlers of Glossop included the Roman legionnaires garrisoned at **★ Melandra Castle** (English Heritage, open all year), the 19-acre (8-hectare) Agricolan fort guarding the western entrance to Longdendale to the northwest of the town, on the edge of the large housing estate at Gamesley. There was also Glott, the Saxon after whom the town is named.

Market day, Old Glossop

Melandra Castle Roman fort

Leave Glossop on the A57, heading west towards Stalybridge and Ashton-under-Lyne, turning right at the traffic lights at Hollingworth, onto the A628 towards Sheffield. Passing through the hamlet of **Tintwistle** (locally pronounced 'Tinsel'), you enter the dramatic cross-Pennine valley of Longdendale, the head of which is known as the Woodhead Pass.

Longdendale has been an important packhorse route across the southern Pennines for centuries. The name of the restored packhorse bridge at Salter's Brook at the head of the pass gives a clue to one of the valuable commodities transported by the horse trains.

The Woodhead Railway, part of the Great Central Railway, was constructed through the valley in 1847 and included the infamous Woodhead Tunnel – at the time the longest in the world. The cost in human suffering of this most difficult route is recalled at the tiny chapel of **★ St James at Woodhead** (just off the A628), where the graves of some of the navvies who lost their lives during the construction of the line can be seen.

The Woodhead line is closed now and redesignated the **★★ Longdendale Trail**, part of the longer Trans-Pennine Trail which links the Irish Sea with the North Sea. The Longdendale Trail is served by a Peak National Park Information Centre at **★★ Torside** (weekends and Bank Holiday Monday, Easter to the end of September) on the B6105 Devil's Elbow minor road from Glossop, near the sailing club on Torside Reservoir.

Another story told at the Torside Centre is that of the string of five reservoirs that fill the valley bottom of Longdendale. When they were built in the late 19th century, they formed the largest man-made expanse of water in the

Longendale: a valley full of reservoirs

world – another great feat of Victorian engineering that was much admired internationally. The reservoirs, from west to east with the years of their construction, are: Bottoms (1869–77), Valehouse (1865–9), Rhodeswood (1849–52), Torside (1849–69) and Woodhead (1848–70). It is a tribute to the Victorian engineer John Bateman that these reservoirs still supply Manchester with nearly 24 million gallons (110 million litres) of water a day.

At **Crowden**, you cross the line of Tom Stephenson's great long-distance path, the **Pennine Way**, which drops down from the peaty heights of **Bleaklow** (2,060ft/633m) to the south to climb the equally boggy wastes of **Black Hill** (1,908ft/582m) to the north, on one of the toughest sections of the Way's 250-mile (400-km) trek up the backbone of England to Kirk Yetholm, just over the Scottish border. Crowden Youth Hostel, to the left of the road, was converted from a long row of cottages by the National Park authority in 1965 to create a vital first overnight stopping place for northbound Pennine Wayfarers.

Crowden Youth Hostel entrance

About a mile past Crowden, turn left on the A6024 towards Holme and Holmfirth. This steep and remote moorland road winds up the valley of the Heyden Brook between Westend Moss (left) and Britland Edge (right) towards the beckoning needle of the **Holme Moss TV transmission mast**, often lost in the lowering clouds. The 725-ft (220-m) mast transmits television pictures over much of this part of northern England, and it stands high on the eastern ridge of Black Hill. There is a car park with fine views extending across the plains to the east.

The road now drops steeply down to the gritstone hamlets of **Holme**, **Holmbridge** and eventually to **Holmfirth**, where the short River Holme flows down from the hills. Like the Etherow in Longdendale, the River Holme and its adjacent streams have been dammed to provide drinking water for the populations beneath. However, when the Bilberry Reservoir was breached in 1852, it caused great devastation and loss of life in the village of Holmfirth, a story which is graphically told in an audio-visual show

WISH YOU WERE HERE . . . .

HOLMFIRTH

Holmfirth Postcard Museum
Sid's Cafe

at the ★★★ **Holmfirth Postcard Museum** (Monday to Saturday 10am–4pm, Sunday noon–4pm), next door to the Tourist **Information Centre** in Huddersfield Road. Bamforth's famous saucy seaside postcards were produced at Holmfirth for many years, and there is a fine collection in the museum. The firm also produced some of the earliest silent films – temporarily turning Holmfirth into a kind of Yorkshire Hollywood.

Holmfirth's modern fame rests on the enduring TV series *Last of the Summer Wine*, which is filmed in the town and the surrounding area. You can visit ★ **Sid's Cafe** and

★ **The Wrinkled Stocking Cafe**, next to ★ **Norah Batty's House**, by the riverside, to relive the adventures of Compo, Foggy and Clegg.

Norah Batty

Leave Holmfirth by the A635 Wessenden Head road, which climbs steeply up to re-enter the National Park at **Harden Moss**, the scene of nationally-famous sheepdog trials in June. This moorland road leads west across **Wessenden Head Moor** to cross the line of the Pennine Way again, which here has been paved with re-cycled slabs from Lancashire cotton mills to prevent the worst effects of erosion on this popular route. Reaching a height of 1,614ft (492m) on the watershed, the road contours down Saddleworth Moor, notorious as the burial site used by the Moors Murderers, on the southern slopes of Hollin Brown Knoll and Dick Hill, with Yeoman Hey and Dove Stone Reservoirs in the valleys below to the left.

Just before you reach Greenfield, take a sharp hairpin left, signposted down to the embankment of the **Dove Stone Reservoir**, where there is plentiful parking. The thriving sailing club based at this beautiful reservoir among the hills has an unusual claim to fame in that it was visited by the King of Tonga in 1953 – he was here for the Queen's Coronation. A good walk from here is to follow the water-works road up the valley of the Chew Brook to reach the windswept Chew Reservoir – the highest in the country at 1,600ft (487m).

Dove Stone Reservoir

Returning to the A635, this is followed to the former mill town of **Greenfield**, then south through **Mossley**, where **Buckton Castle** (no access) above the quarries on Buckton Moor was probably a small Iron Age fortification commanding the valley of the River Tame. At **Stalybridge**, a busy little town named after the medieval bridge built by the Stayley family from Millbrook, turn left on the A6108 to **Mottram in Longdendale**. Mottram's ★ **parish church** (mainly 15th-century) dominates the village from War Hill overlooking the jaws of Longdendale. Local tradition states that it was originally built on the site of a medieval battle, hence the name of the hill. War Hill is a fine viewpoint, and the churchyard has some interesting memorials.

Mottram parish church

Mottram was the former home of the noted northern artist L.S. Lowry, who lived alone here from 1948 until he died in 1976. His mainly industrial landscapes of Manchester and the North-West often included the misty moors of the Pennines in the background, and he was well-known as a local 'character'.

Turning left onto the A628 again, you descend back down into Hollingworth, then right on the A57 through **Dinting Vale** under the splendid Dinting Railway Viaduct and back to your starting point in Glossop.

Route 2

The Wild West

Macclesfield – Poynton – Hazel Grove – Lyme Park – Whaley Bridge – Goyt Valley – Buxton – The Roaches – Leek – Gawsworth – Macclesfield (56 miles / 90km)

Macclesfield: prosperity based on silk

Approaching the Peak District from the Cheshire Plain and the west, visitors can have no doubt that they are entering hill country. The western edge of the Pennines rears up suddenly from the lowlands, punctuated by dramatic rocky ridges like that of The Roaches, above Leek, and the wild moorland heights of the Goyt Valley above its tranquil reservoirs.

Beyond those heights, secret valleys like that of the River Dane and the Clough and Todd Brooks, wind into the hills, creating a landscape of myth and mystery where larger-than-life legends linger on, and ancient traditions survive the bustle of the 20th century.

All this is never far from industrial towns like Macclesfield, Leek and Congleton, which owe their wealth to the mills that worked silk and cotton, powered by the waters rushing down from the moors to the east. Add to this fascinating mixture the attraction of the country houses and estates of Lyme Park, and Gawsworth and Little Moreton Halls, and it's easy to see why the 'Wild West' of the Peak District has so many devotees.

Medieval **Macclesfield** was granted a charter to establish a free borough as early as 1261 by Edward I. This enabled the burgesses of the little town above the valley of the Bollin to establish a merchant guild, set up courts and hold regular markets. Before that, the town was the administrative centre for the medieval hunting forest of Macclesfield, which belonged to Ranulf, Earl of Chester. The serried ranks of the Forestry Commission's conifers in the hills above the town are the only echo of that history.

Macclesfield's modern fame rests on the silk industry that was

brought to the town in 1742 by Charles Roe, a noted burgess. Three excellent museums tell the story of Macclesfield's rise to fame as a major producer of what is described here as 'the world's most luxurious fabric'.

The best place to start is the ★★ **Macclesfield Heritage Centre** in Roe Street (Monday to Saturday 11am–5pm, Sunday 1pm–5pm), which also houses the ★★★ **Silk Museum**. Here, in a restored Sunday School, is the only museum in the country dedicated to the silk industry. There is also a shop and the aptly-named Mulberry Tree Restaurant. The last handloom weaver in Macclesfield retired in 1981, when Cartwright and Sheldon's Paradise Mill in Park Lane closed, but the visitor can see 25 working Jacquard handlooms at the ★★★ **Paradise Mill Working Silk Museum** (Tuesday to Saturday 1pm–5pm, except November to March, 1–4pm), which is a few minutes' walk from the Silk Museum.

Spinning and weaving at Paradise Mill

An interesting way of exploring Macclesfield's silken past is to follow the Silk Trail. A leaflet is available from the **Tourist Information Centre** at the Town Hall (Monday to Thursday 8.45am–5pm, 4.30pm on Friday).

Leave Macclesfield by the A523 dual carriageway Poynton Road, which heads north in the valley of the River Bollin to reach the town of Poynton, now a suburb of Stockport but with a fascinating industrial history of its own, told in the ★ **Anson Museum** (only open Sunday 11am–5pm, May to October). The ★ **Poynton Inclines** once linked local coal mines with the Macclesfield Canal and the railway (now closed).

Entering **Hazel Grove**, turn right at the traffic lights onto the A6 towards Buxton. Passing through Disley, signs to the right indicate ★★★ **Lyme Park** (National Trust with Stockport Borough Council; hall open April to September Saturday to Wednesday 1.30–5pm; park open daily

Macclesfield Canal

Red deer in Lyme Park

Inn and barge at Whaley Bridge

Taxal parish church

from 8am all year). Lyme is one of the Peak District's most impressive stately homes. Originally built by the Legh family in Tudor times, the present Palladian mansion was designed by Leoni in 1720, and its three-storey Ionic portico on the south front is reflected by a peaceful lake. The interior is famous for its intricate carvings by Grinling Gibbons, its clock collection and its beautiful ★★ **Orangery**, but Lyme Park's latest claim to fame has been as a location for the BBC's 1995 television adaptation of Jane Austen's *Pride and Prejudice*. The extensive 1,320-acre (534-hectare) ★ **Park** is famous for its herd of red deer, the largest in the Peak District, and it backs onto the moorland of Park Moor, where the hunting tower known as the **Cage** is a prominent landmark.

Leaving Lyme Park, go back onto the A6 and turn right, passing through **Newtown** and **Furness Vale** along the Goyt Valley. Increasingly fine views open out to the east toward the highest point of the Peak District, Kinder Scout. After about 2 miles (3km), enter the busy little township of **Whaley Bridge**.

Whaley Bridge retains the atmosphere of an early industrial town with a railway and canal threading the narrow valley. It used to be the northern terminus of the Cromford and High Peak Railway, now part of the High Peak Trail, and the railway's junction with the Peak Forest Canal. Colourful narrowboats can usually be seen moored in the canal basin at Whaley Bridge, but they are used for pleasure, rather than commerce. The Cromford and High Peak Railway had to descend 750ft (228m) by four inclines from the Goyt Moors, the most famous of which was the Bunsall Cob incline, now followed by the minor road which leads down into the Goyt Valley from the A5004. The final incline down into Whaley Bridge was operated by a horse gin.

From the centre of Whaley Bridge, follow the A5004 to the crossroads at **Horwich End**. Here you cross over the B5470, which turns left towards Chapel-en-le-Frith, whose name literally translates to 'the chapel in the forest' – the forest in question being the medieval Royal Forest of the Peak District.

Soon after leaving Horwich End, the road passes the small hamlet of ★ **Taxal**, over the river to the right as the road climbs out of the valley. Taxal is a much older settlement than industrial Whaley Bridge, and its parish church and graveyard continue to serve the larger township downstream. The A5004 continues to climb through the hamlet of Fernilee and it eventually leads out onto the moors, offering splendid views down to the right across the **Fernilee Reservoir** with the wooded heights of Hoo Moor leading up to Cats Tor beyond.

Negotiate the hairpin at Rake End and further sharp bends which take the road past the White Hall Outdoor Pursuits Centre (left among the trees), then watch for signs to the Goyt Valley down a minor road to the right.

The right turn is very sharp and the descent steep into the ★★★ **Goyt Valley**. This was the route of the Bunsall Cob incline (*see page 22*), and there are increasingly lovely views down the length of the **Fernilee Reservoir** and **Errwood Reservoir** ahead. The Goyt Valley reservoirs came late in the history of Peak District reservoir building. The Fernilee was built in 1938 and the Errwood only in 1967, both to supply water for Stockport.

Such was the popularity of this man-made landscape that in 1970 the National Park authority introduced a pioneering road-closure scheme, still in operation on summer weekends, which bans cars from the upper reaches of the valley. However, there was another, heavier, price to be paid for flooding the Goyt – the demolition of the Italianate pile of Errwood Hall, home of the Grimshawe family since it was built in 1830. The Grimshawes were great travellers, and the massed ranks of rhododendrons and azaleas that now flank the western shores of the Errwood Reservoir, site of a thriving yachting club, are the result of their collecting.

Goyt Valley leisure pursuits

After parking in the large National Park car park and picnic area at Errwood, take a Forest Trail up through the trees to the forlorn ruins of what is left of ★★ **Errwood Hall**. Higher up is the Errwood family graveyard and the small circular chapel or shrine, which was built in memory of a popular Spanish governess to the family.

You now have a choice of routes. You can return to the A5004 by Bunsall Cob, turning right for Buxton via Long Hill. Alternatively, the route can be shortened by following the valley road through the Goyt (weekdays only in summer because of the traffic scheme) up past Derbyshire Bridge and across Goyt's Moss to the **Cat and Fiddle Road** (A537). Turn right past the eponymous pub – at 1,690ft (515m) it is the second-highest in England and a fine viewpoint – and drop down into Macclesfield in about 5 miles (8km). This choice offers fine views across the Cheshire Plain to the dish of **Jodrell Bank Radio Telescope** in the distance near Lower Withington.

The main route rejoins the A5004, climbs Long Hill then descends steeply into **Buxton** (*see page 25*). Turn right at the first roundabout onto the A53 Leek road, which leads out through Burbage and up onto the moors beneath Axe Edge. This former Roman Road from Buxton (Aquae Arnemetiae) climbs steadily, with views to the Upper Dove valley to the left, where the jagged limestone hills of Chrome and Parkhouse are prominent.

Close-up view of Jodrell Bank

The Roaches

Leek: the Market Place

A plaque recalls the past

JAMES
BRINDLEY
CANAL ENGINEER
worked here
1742-1765

Gawsworth Hall

The road passes the scattered hamlet of **Flash**, at 1,518ft (463m) said to be the highest village in England. It is also allegedly the source of the term 'flash money', for it was once the headquarters of a band of counterfeit coiners. Nearby on the moors is the packhorse bridge at **Three Shires Head**, where the three counties of Derbyshire, Cheshire and Staffordshire meet, and where bare-knuckle prize fights used to be staged, well away from the prying eyes of authority.

At **Royal Cottage**, a public house said to be named after the visit of Bonnie Prince Charlie in 1745, the road starts to drop down past the jagged gritstone teeth of ★★ **Ramshaw Rocks** to the right (see if you can spot the outcrop known as the Winking Man). Ramshaw Rocks is a great place for children to explore, as are the safe paths above ★★★ **The Roaches**, which are reached by turning right off the A53 at **Upper Hulme**.

The Roaches (derived from the French word for rocks) is one of the most famous and popular rock climbing areas in the Peak District, but equally popular with walkers for the fine views across the Cheshire Plain to the distant Mersey. Halfway along the minor road (limited parking) below The Roaches can be seen the romantically-sited Rock Hall cottage, built partly into the rock as a shooting cabin and now used as a bothy for climbers. **Hen Cloud** (1,240ft/378m) is an isolated outlier from the main Roaches syncline, offering more fine climbing and excellent views. The Roaches estate is owned by the National Park authority, and at summer weekends, a park and ride bus service runs from **Tittesworth Reservoir**.

Drop down into **Leek**, a busy market town known as the Capital of the Moorlands and, like Macclesfield, a former silk and cotton town. Leek was granted a charter in 1208 to hold a market, and the cobbled ★★ **Market Place**, complete with Butter Cross dating from the 17th century, is a little gem overlooked by many. The ★★ **Brindley Mill and Museum** (Easter to end of October, weekends and Bank Holidays, also Monday, Tuesday and Wednesday from the third Monday in July to the end of August, 2–5pm) in Mill Street is a restored water-powered corn mill originally built by the great canal engineer James Brindley in 1752. It is well worth a visit.

From Leek take the A523 back to Macclesfield past **Rudyard Reservoir** to the left (after which, apparently, the great Victorian author Rudyard Kipling was named), through **Rushden Spencer** to cross the A54 near Bosley. About a mile further on, signs lead left to ★★ **Gawsworth Hall** a late 15th-century, black and white, half-timbered manor house (Easter to end of October). Macclesfield is about 3 miles (5km) to the north.

Route 3

A walk around Buxton

Spring Gardens – The Crescent – St Ann's Well – Opera House – Pavilion – St John's Church – The Slopes – Market Place – Museum and Art Gallery *See map on page 26*

The 5th Duke of Devonshire's 'Grand Design' to make Buxton a spa to rival Bath and Cheltenham never quite captured the public imagination, although it did enjoy modest popularity in the 18th and 19th centuries.

Unlike the more fashionable southern spas, Buxton's northern geography was always going to be a disadvantage. Buxton is one of Britain's highest market towns (the Market Place stands at over 1,000ft/300m), and its frequently severe winters make it one of the first towns to be cut off when the snows arrive.

However, there are many proud and impressive echoes of Buxton's fascinating past still to be seen, from the sweeping vista of Carr's recently-renovated Crescent opposite St Ann's Well, to the ornate Edwardian Opera House and soaring dome of the Great Stables, now the Royal Devonshire Hospital. As is often the case with British spas, it was the Romans who were first attracted by the constant 28°C (82°F) thermal springs found in the town, and they named their spa *Aquae Arnemetiae* – which means the Spa of the Goddess of the Grove. Roman finds can be seen in the excellent town museum.

This short stroll around the centre of Buxton takes in most of the points of interest and can easily be accomplished in a morning or afternoon.

Echoes of Buxton's past: Pavilion…

…and Town Hall

25

Carnival comes to town

The Crescent

The Lord Mayor

26

Start from the large pay-and-display car park behind Spring Gardens, the main shopping thoroughfare of Buxton. Across the New Relief Road can be seen the railway line, which reached Buxton in 1863. There are plans to reopen the former Midland line through the heart of the Peak District to Matlock by a group called Peak Rail, which occasionally runs steam trains for a short distance along the old line to the east of the station.

Walk through the modern shopping precinct to emerge onto Spring Gardens, turning right towards the town centre and the green bank of The Slopes.

Note the ornate Victorian ironwork colonnade at the junction of Spring Gardens and Bridge Street, and also opposite in Bridge Street. Cross by the traffic lights to get a first view of the elegant ★★★ **Crescent ❶** (not open to the public), now beautifully restored following many years of sad neglect.

The Crescent was built between 1780 and 1784 on the orders of the 5th Duke of Devonshire to offer high-class accommodation and assembly rooms as part of his master plan to make Buxton a fashionable spa town. He commissioned the famous York architect John Carr to design the magnificent building, and he modelled it on John Wood's Royal Crescent at Bath. The total cost of the Corinthian-style arcaded building was £120,000 – an astonishing sum for those days. Folklore has it that the Duke paid for the Crescent using the profits from his copper mines at Ecton Hill in Staffordshire.

There were three hotels in the original design – the Grand, the Crescent and St Ann's – and each had private entrances to the baths beneath and shops on the arcaded ground floor. ★★ **The Assembly Rooms**, once used for

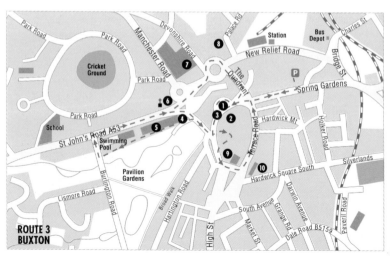

ROUTE 3 BUXTON

church services and later to become a geriatrics hospital, have now been restored as part of the public library. It has a magnificent Adam-style ceiling. **★★ The Thermal Baths**, on the right, were converted into the Cavendish Shopping Arcade, but they retain a plunge pool complete with bosun's chair-type seat showing how some patients were encouraged to 'take the waters'.

The Cavendish Arcade

Opposite the Crescent is the low classical structure built in 1894 as part of the spa development and known as **The Pump Room ❷**, which until recently housed a fascinating Micrarium, showing the world of nature through the microscope. This is now unfortunately closed. The warm waters could be seen gushing from the rock in this elegant building, which also had a dispensing pool, but it is now closed to the public.

The visitor can, however, still use the drinking fountain outside, known locally as **★★ St Ann's Well** and the scene during July of one of the town's well-dressings (*see page 64*), a tradition that was revived in 1840. Visitors can sample the warm, blue and slightly effervescent spring water here freely, and there are often queues of people waiting to fill containers with the precious liquid. The fountain was presented to the town in 1940 as a memorial to a local councillor.

Well-dressing at St Ann's Well

Buxton's Tourist Information Centre is housed in **★★ The Natural Baths ❸**, left of the Crescent, where there is an interpretive display showing the origins of the thermal waters. It is appropriately sponsored by Buxton Mineral Water.

Walk past the Natural Baths and up to the corner of The Square, where massive gritstone 'cloisters' face the attractive Pavilion Gardens, laid out along the banks of the infant River Wye in 1871, when the Pavilion was built. Turn right at this corner, where the Old Hall Hotel marks the site of Buxton Old Hall, originally dating from 1530 but rebuilt in 1670 and Buxton's oldest building. Mary Queen of Scots frequently stayed at Buxton Old Hall when she took the waters for her chronic rheumatism while she was being detained at Chatsworth and Sheffield. She is reputed to have scratched the following message on a window with her ring on her final visit in 1582:

> *Buxton, whose fame thy milkwarm waters tell,*
> *Whom I perhaps shall see no more, farewell.*

Turning up the Square, you are faced with the ornate, twin-domed frontage of **★★★ The Opera House ❹**, (box office open Monday to Saturday 10am–6pm). Designed and built in the grand Edwardian style by the eminent theatrical architect Frank Matcham in 1905, the Opera House was

Opera House performance

sensitively restored to its former opulence in 1979, after serving for many years as a cinema.

Inside, the theatre seats nearly 1,000 people in a magnificently decorated auditorium, with a large and richly ornamented proscenium arch flanked by beautiful boxes and lit by a massive and unusual gas-fired crystal chandelier. This 'Theatre in the Hills' is now the home of the widely-acclaimed Buxton International Festival of Music and the Arts, held annually at the end of July.

The Opera House stages a varied programme of comedy, drama, ballet, children's shows and concerts, as well as opera, throughout the year, and it is a favourite of many visiting artists and a tribute to the many local people behind its magnificent restoration.

Turning left in front of the Opera House, walk past the splendid Victorian ★★ **Pavilion** ❺, built in 1871 by Edward Milner on instructions from the Duke of Devonshire. The **Conservatory** is passed first, a light and airy concoction of glass and steel that houses a variety of tropical and native plants and a small aviary. In the centre of the Pavilion is the superb **Octagon** or Concert Hall, designed by R.R. Duke and opened in 1876, which soars above the Pavilion Gardens from a classical facade. The Pavilion is well supplied with restaurants, bars and lounges and is used for various events from antique and book fairs to wrestling matches in its variety of halls. Just beyond the Octagon is the large modern swimming pool, filled with naturally warm spa water.

★★ **The Pavilion Gardens**, also laid out by Milner, provide 23 acres (9 hectares) of pleasantly landscaped gardens by the banks of the River Wye. There are Serpentine Walks, two lakes, a large children's play area, putting greens, crazy golf and a miniature railway that encircles the smaller lake.

Inside the Conservatory

Aspects of the Pavilion Gardens

Although the Pavilion Gardens continue beyond Burlington Road, turn right into St John's Road to walk behind the Pavilion to the ★★ **Parish Church of St John the Baptist** , a beautiful example of Italianate Georgian architecture standing in an oasis of green. The building of the parish church was in many ways the spiritual culmination of the redevelopments by the 6th Duke of Devonshire (the 'Bachelor Duke'). Designed by Sir Jeffrey Wyatville, who worked with him at Chatsworth, it is built in a Tuscan style and contains some fine mosaics and stained glass behind a massive portico and under an elegant tower rising to a copper dome.

Beyond the parish church, on rising ground beyond the Manchester Road, is the great dome of ★★ **the Devonshire Royal Hospital** ❼ (closed to the public). This was formerly the Great Stables, built in 1790 by Carr to house the horses of visitors to the spa. In 1859 it was converted to a hospital following designs by R.R. Duke. The great dome that so dominates Buxton was begun in 1880, at which time it was the widest unsupported iron-framed dome in the world, spanning 152ft (46m). It was an architectural wonder of the age.

Devonshire Royal Hospital

Across Devonshire Road from the hospital stands the imposing facade of ★★ **The Palace Hotel** ❽, Buxton's largest and most prestigious hotel, built at the height of the resort's popularity in 1868 to designs by Henry Currey. It stands close to the ★ **London and North Western Railway Station**, of which unfortunately only the facade remains, with its great semi-circular fan window.

Returning to the route, walk down The Quadrant back to The Crescent and the steep paths that wind up ★★ **The Slopes** ❾, laid out by Wyatville to provided graded paths for exercise, and probably also to improve the view from The Crescent. At the top of The Slopes, which offer fine views across the town, is the ★ **Town Hall**, designed by William Pollard and opened in 1889.

Hall Bank is the steep street leading up from The Slopes to the Market Place and the area known as Higher Buxton, where the weekly street market is held.

Hall Bank seen from The Slopes

Turn left down Terrace Road from the Market Place to visit ★★★ **Buxton Museum and Art Gallery** ❿ halfway down on the right (all year, Tuesday to Friday, 9.30am–5.30pm; Saturday 9.30am–5pm; Sunday and Bank Holidays from Easter to the end of September, 10.30am–5pm). This is an excellent example of a small museum, with an award-winning display entitled *The Wonders of the Peak*, which takes the visitor back in a time-tunnel complete with sounds and smells. There are also art galleries and an excellent museum shop.

Descend the hill to turn right, back into Spring Gardens.

Museum and Art Gallery

Sheffield Town Hall entrance

National Park Ranger

Cathedral Church of St Mary:
sculpture detail

Route 4

Sheffield's Golden Frame

**Sheffield – Langsett – High and Low Bradfield – La-
dybower – Bamford – Hathersage – North Lees Hall
– Stanage Edge – Grindleford – Froggatt – Sheffield
(48 miles / 77km)** *See map on pages 14–15*

Sheffield, Britain's fifth largest city and the former base
of its steel industry, is justly proud of its 'Golden Frame'.
Few British cities have such a wealth of beautiful countryside on their doorsteps, and none other in Europe has
part of a National Park within its borders.

The moors and dales of the Peak District have long held
a special place in the affections of the people of the Steel
City, and generations of foundry workers found their weekend release walking and climbing in the Peak.

Many of the prosperous villages that lie beneath the
Eastern Moors in the sheltered valley of the River Derwent look towards Sheffield for their services and employment, but it was not always so. The power of the
mighty Derwent was harnessed in a series of mills, like
those at Bamford and Calver, as industry first came to
the Peak. And on the steep, cliff-like 'edges' on the east
flank of the Derwent Valley, another industry once flour-
ished serving the famous Sheffield cutlery factories. Stacks
of part-finished mill and grindstones can still be found,
gradually being buried under the bracken.

Some of the Peak District's most famous families made
their home in the Derwent Valley, like the Eyres who came
to England with the Conqueror. And their halls, like North
Lees and Padley, looked out over the peaceful pastures
leading down to the Derwent.

The route starts from the centre of **Sheffield**, a city emerging from the double decline of the steel industry and the closure of South Yorkshire collieries. The city council has an enlightened attitude to public transport, most recently manifested in the return of tramcars to the city streets with the advent of the Supertram.

Supertram

A lively cultural scene is reflected in the excellent museums, among the most interesting of which is the ★★★ **Sheffield City Museum and Mappin Art Gallery** at Weston Park on the A57 Glossop Road (open all year, Tuesday to Saturday 10am–5pm, Sunday and Bank Holiday Monday 11am–5pm). The majority of the most important archaeological finds in the Peak District – notably the Bateman collection – is held here. Don't miss the famous Anglo-Saxon Benty Grange helmet, one of only a handful ever found in Britain, with its beautifully-reconstructed replica. There are also natural history exhibits, and the adjoining Mappin Art Gallery has a fine collection of the work of local artists.

City Museum and Art Gallery

The ★★ **Ruskin Gallery** in Norfolk Street (Monday to Saturday 10am–5pm) includes the collection of the Guild of St George, the movement started by John Ruskin in 1870 to show working-class people the finest in art and nature.

31

★★ **Abbeydale Industrial Hamlet** (Tuesday to Saturday and Bank Holidays 10am–5pm, Sunday 11am–5pm) on Abbeydale Road South (A621) is a living museum of Sheffield's industrial past. Working days are held regularly (watch for advertisements), and craftsmen return to show their traditional skills in this restored water-powered scythe and steelworks. Abbeydale includes a crucible steel furnace, workman's cottage and four working waterwheels, all in a delightful wooded setting by the River Sheaf.

Industrial heritage at Abbeydale

Leave Sheffield by the A61 Penistone Road, turning onto the A6102 Stocksbridge road at Hillsborough to follow the wooded valley of the River Don through Oughtibridge and Wharncliffe. At the junction with the A616 east of Stocksbridge, turn left (west) around this industrial town and climb up past the Underbank Reservoir to reach the village of **Langsett**.

Langsett (the name means long slope) is a village at an important crossroads of ancient trans-Pennine routes and now cruelly at the mercy of endless processions of heavy lorries. Its former agricultural importance is reflected in the lovely 17th-century ★★ **Langsett Barn**, which was recently restored and converted into a community hall, information centre (Easter to end of September, weekends and Bank Holiday Monday) and ranger base. There is a large car park and waymarked walks lead

Langsett Barn

Moors between Langsett and Bradfield

St Nicholas in High Bradfield

Strines Inn

around the **★★ Langsett Reservoir**, built to serve Sheffield and Barnsley with water but now also a pleasant local attraction. Longer walks follow a famous packhorse route known as the Cut Gate Track, which leads across the bleak Langsett Moors to the Derwent Valley.

From Langsett, follow the signs to the Derwent Valley on the minor road across the Langsett Dam wall, whose tower with battlements was apparently modelled on Lancaster Castle. At the road junction beyond the dam, turn right following the signs to Derwent. This is the Strines Road, which contours in and out of the valleys running down off the moors to the east towards Sheffield.

Many of these valleys, like that of the Little Don at Langsett, have been flooded for reservoirs, and you soon pass Broomhead Reservoir in the valley of the Ewden Beck, nestling among its cloak of conifers to the left. Broomhead Hall, now demolished, once loomed from behind the long estate wall to the left of the road, a Victorian mansion built by a Sheffield entrepreneur. Each of the reservoirs, mostly built in the early years of the 20th century, attracted its own community of navvies, who lived in model villages like that at nearby **Ewden Village** while work was under way.

As the road climbs up across Broomhead Moor, fork left at a junction towards Bradfield. The road crosses the mysterious **★★ Bar Dyke**, a deep entrenchment thought to be a boundary ditch dating from the Dark Ages.

The road drops down to the pretty gritstone village of **High Bradfield** where, in the fields to the right of the road can be seen the prominent circular mound of Bailey Hill, the remains of a Norman motte-and-bailey castle built to guard the upper reaches of the Loxley Valley. The beautiful and commanding **★★ Parish Church of St Nicholas** dates mainly from the 15th century but has a 14th-century pinnacled and castellated tower. The view down the valley to the Agden and Damflask Reservoirs across the patchwork fields to the distant moors from the south porch is one of the finest in the Peak. An unusual feature is the 18th-century **★★ Watch House** (private) which was built to guard against the menace of the body-snatchers intent on plundering the graveyard.

Pass through the village of **Low Bradfield** (usually referred to simply as Bradfield), which shelters under the embankment of the Agden Reservoir, turning right at the junction to rise steeply beside the reservoir. Turn left at the next junction to pass through a conifer plantation above the Dale Dike and Strines Reservoirs. A hairpin bend above Strines Bridge leads to the **★★ Strines Inn**, a famous moorland hostelry which is reputed to date from the 14th century.

Follow the Strines Road south to its junction with the A57 at Moscar Lodge, turning right to head down towards the **Ladybower Reservoir**, passing Cutthroat Bridge on the right, where a brutal murder is said to have been committed in the 16th century.

Turn left onto the A6013, passing the huge embankment wall of the Ladybower Dam, completed in 1945 opposite the now disused treatment works for the Derwent Dams. Just past here on the left is the public house and hamlet of **Yorkshire Bridge**, where villagers from the drowned villages of Derwent and Ashopton were rehoused after the construction of the Ladybower Dam.

Bamford's ★ Parish Church is in elegant Victorian gothic style, built in 1860 and best-known for the fact that the deceased villagers of Derwent were re-interred in the churchyard. **Bamford Mill**, in trees on the right as you leave the village, was established as a cotton mill in 1780. Today, after a chequered history, it is being converted to residential use. After about half a mile (0.8km), the A625 main Hope Valley road is reached at the Marquis of Granby pub. Turn left towards Sheffield and Hathersage.

Hathersage is a prosperous and busy village on the edge of the Sheffield commuter range and is perhaps best-known for its legendary connections with Robin Hood's loyal friend, Little John. This is reflected in an inn sign just off the main road by a beautifully-restored Edwardian lamp standard, and in a conveniently-long 'grave' in the churchyard of the hilltop **★★ Parish Church**. No-one will ever prove the gravestone is correct and this 10-ft (3-m) long grave really is John Little's, a Hathersage nailor. Nail-making and later wire-drawing to produce pins and needles was a Hathersage trade, and many local men were employed in making mill and grindstones from the nearby gritstone edges like Stanage, overlooking the village.

Bamford Parish Church

The Little John in Hathersage

33

Ladybower Reservoir

Stunts at Stanage Edge

Stanage: a mecca for climbers

★★ **Stanage Edge** can be reached by a minor road that leads northeast out of the village up the valley of the Hood Brook. This passes close to the imposing Tudor tower house of ★★ **North Lees Hall** (private), one of the seven halls in this locality attributed to Thomas Eyre. North Lees Hall is also thought to have been used by Charlotte Brontë as the model for Thornfield Hall in her novel *Jane Eyre*. She is known to have stayed with her friend Ellen Nussey at Hathersage Vicarage in 1845.

There is a car park beneath the frowning crags of Stanage Edge, one of the most impressive of the Peak District edges and a magnet for rock climbers from all over Britain. But the great appeal of Stanage is that it offers climbs of all grades of difficulty, so novices come here as well. Climbers share their sport on the 4-mile (6-km) edge with colourful hangliders.

Returning to Hathersage, take the valley road (B6001) past the station and over the River Derwent to **Grindleford**. This is a straggling village along the banks of the Derwent, but at **Upper Padley**, a rough track opposite the Maynard Arms leads past the station to ★★ **Padley Chapel** (April to September Sunday and Wednesday 2–4pm). This early 14th-century gatehouse and chapel is all that remains of Padley Manor House, the home of two Roman Catholic families who were persecuted. Two priests were taken from here and executed in 1588.

From Grindleford, stay on the B6001 valley road towards the village of **Calver**, where the mill (private) originally built in 1805 was used as a set for the TV series *Colditz*, and turn left on the B6054 towards Sheffield. This road passes through the commuter village of **Froggatt** and under the crags of **Froggatt Edge** to return across the moors to Sheffield via the A625.

Route 5

The Upper Derwent and Snake Pass

Glossop – Snake Pass – Alport Valley – Ladybower –
the Upper Derwent Valley – Fairholmes – Derwent –
Howden – Hallam Moors – Sheffield (35 miles / 56km)
See map on pages 14–5

The A57 Snake Pass road across the Pennines between
Sheffield and Manchester is well-known from winter
weather warnings on the radio. It is always one of the
first roads to be closed and the last to reopen. This is because it is one of the highest – it reaches 1,680ft (512m)
at the summit – and most exposed motor roads in Britain.
The tall snow posts that line the highest stretch between
Kinder Scout and Bleaklow are often needed to trace the
road when it is buried in the drifts, and even a light scat-
tering of snow on either side of the pass can mean that
the road will be closed on top.

*Arrivals at the Snake Pass,
Bleaklow in the background* **35**

The road takes its name not, as some have supposed,
from the winding and circuitous nature of the route up
Holden Clough and down Lady Clough to the Woodlands
Valley. It comes from the serpent that crowns the coat of
arms of the Duke of Devonshire, a major landowner locally and chairman of the Snake turnpike trust.

Just off the Snake Road as it descends into the Woodlands Valley is the Alport Valley, which winds into the
heart of Bleaklow past one of the largest landslips in
Britain. From the conifers of Woodlands Valley, a minor
road which is closed to traffic at busy times leads north
deep into the hills past the twin reservoirs of the Derwent and Howden – the famous Derwent Dams.

Beyond the Ladybower Reservoir, the third of the series that floods the Upper Derwent Valley, the road climbs
over the bleak Hallam Moors and down into the Rivelin
Valley to Sheffield.

Take the A57 from the centre of Glossop (*see page 16*)
towards Sheffield. The Snake Road here follows the line
of **Doctor's Gate**, a Roman road which linked the forts
at Melandra (*see page 17*) in Glossop with Navio (*see page
42*) at Brough in the Hope Valley. It takes its name from
Dr John Talbot, a Glossop vicar and schoolmaster who
regularly used this route in the 17th century.

A well-trodden path

Passing Glossop Golf Club on the right, the road winds
up around the wooded southern slopes of quarry-scarred
Shire Hill (left) to the hairpin at Mossy Lea. It is now a
steep rise up Coldharbour Moor, leaving behind the glint-
ing eye of the Hurst Reservoir backed by the chimneys
of industrial Glossop beyond.

The road runs high above Holden Clough, with the peat hags and groughs of Featherbed Moss over to the right. It levels out at the 1,680-ft (512-m) summit of the **Snake Pass**, marked by a small tarn on the left and the unmistakable line of the **Pennine Way**, crossed here at a pair of ladder stiles. Such is the serious erosion on this popular wilderness route, sections of it here have been paved with gritstone slabs recycled from demolished local mills and airlifted in by helicopter by the authorities.

This crossing is on one of the toughest sections of Britain's hardest long-distance path. The walker, having floundered through the hags and groughs of Kinder Scout, Mill Hill and Featherbed Moss to the south, must now negotiate the equally-sticky and notorious peat bogs of Bleaklow to the north before descending to the relative comforts of Longdendale.

Snake Pass: moor meets dale

From the Snake Summit, the road swings down in a series of sharp bends into Lady Clough, where the first plantations of conifers which now cloak the Woodlands Valley are encountered. After about a mile (1.5km) the isolated hostelry known as ★★ **The Snake Inn**, a welcome and sometimes life-saving landmark for walkers and travellers, is reached on the left, sheltering under the strangely-named Dinas Sitch Tor in the trees above. The Snake Inn was built in 1821 as a posting house on the Glossop to Sheffield turnpike – one of the last to be opened in the country.

36

The Snake Inn

The conifers of the Snake Plantation now disappear, and the road enters open country again, punctuated by isolated farms and, to the right, increasingly fine views of the prominent prow of Fairbrook Naze and Seal and Blackden Edges, the northern ramparts of **Kinder Scout** – at 2,088ft (636m) the highest point in the Peak District.

There is a small amount of car parking near Blackden Barn, from where, walking down the road for about half a mile (0.8km) and crossing at Hayridge Farm, access on foot can be gained to one of the hidden gems of the Peak District – the **Alport Dale**. A farm track leads up for about a mile (1.5km) to Alport Castles Farm (private) where, on the first Sunday of July, a unique 'Love Feast' is held in an adjacent barn. This recalls the banning of nonconformist preaching in Charles II's reign (1660–85), and commemorates the use of makeshift places of worship like this barn by preachers such as John Wesley, far from the prying eyes of the authorities. Lookouts would keep watch on the neighbouring hills while the services were held. Today's Love Feast is a simple but moving ceremony consisting of people giving personal testimonies, singing hymns and sharing cakes and spring water.

Frowning down above the farm high on the side of the dale to the east are the dramatic towers and cliffs of

★★ **Alport Castles**, reputedly the largest landslip in the country. The layers of gritstone and shales are very unstable, and are constantly falling away. They have left behind them the tottering Tower and a chaotic jumble of boulders which, from a distance, are said to resemble a ruinous castle. A steep footpath, which should only be attempted by fit and experienced walkers, leads up from the farm across a footbridge and passes the southern end of Alport Castles.

Back on the A57, the road passes the isolated **Woodlands Chapel** on the left, built for his tenants by the 7th Duke of Devonshire. The road now enters the trees again, passing Hagg Farm, high on the left, formerly a youth hostel and now used for outdoor pursuits by Nottinghamshire County Council.

The western arm of the **Ladybower Reservoir** now appears in the valley bottom to the right. This was the last to be built in the Upper Derwent, in 1935–45, and is by far the largest, holding over 6 billion gallons. It is well stocked with fish and very popular with anglers, who are often seen along its shores.

As the road approaches the white-painted Ashopton Viaduct, a sign points left into the Derwent Valley. The ★★★ **Upper Derwent Valley** is a place quite unlike anywhere else in the Peak District. Despite the fact that most of the landscape is entirely man-made – from the reservoirs and dams to the banks of conifers that surround them – it is extremely popular with visitors. So popular, in fact, that since the early 1980s an award-winning traffic management scheme had to be introduced to cope with the ever-increasing volume of traffic that was choking the narrow cul-de-sac road. Now, at weekends and Bank Holidays, the road north of Fairholmes is closed to traffic, and minibus and cycle-hire services are provided. It is a popular and innovative solution by the many people who live in, work and manage the valley.

The Upper Derwent Valley and some of its woodland

What makes the Upper Derwent such a popular destination? In addition to the artificial but still magnificent scenery, few places have such fascinating stories to tell. They are told in the small but informative ★★★ **National Park Visitor Centre at Fairholmes** (Easter to the end of October daily 10.30am–5.30pm; winter, weekends only 10.30am–5pm; times may vary), about 2 miles (3km) north of the junction with the A57.

Many visitors are intrigued by the story of the two villages, **Derwent** and **Ashopton**, that had to be sacrificed under the rising waters of the Ladybower Reservoir. The interest runs particularly high when drought conditions reveal the foundations of Derwent village in the northern arm of the reservoir.

Among the buildings that were demolished and de-populated were Derwent Hall, a stately Jacobean mansion that became a shooting lodge used by the Duke of Norfolk and later one of the first youth hostels in the Peak District, and the parish church of St John and St James, with its elegant broached spire. An ancient packhorse bridge that crossed the Derwent near the hall was taken down and reassembled at ★★ **Slippery Stones**, beyond the northern end of the valley road, which can be reached by a short walk from **King's Tree**.

The motorist passes over the site of Ashopton village when crossing the Ashopton Viaduct on the A57. Ashopton was an important staging post on the turnpike linking Glossop and Sheffield, and horses were changed at the Ashopton Inn, built in 1824. Ashopton also boasted one of the finest Methodist chapels in the Peak District.

Dambuster display and memorial

Among the lasting stories of the Derwent is that of Tip the sheepdog, which faithfully remained by the body of its owner Joseph Tagg for 15 weeks when he died in a winter snowstorm in 1953. ★★ **Tip's Memorial** is by the western tower of the Derwent Dam, attached to which is another tale of heroism. Because of the similarity between the Derwent Dams and those of the Ruhr of Hitler's Germany, the valley was used for training purposes by 617 Squadron – the Dambusters – before their epic 'bouncing bomb' raid in 1943. Subsequent anniversary flypasts over the reservoir by the last flying Lancaster bomber have attracted huge crowds.

Derwent Dam

The ★★★ **Derwent and Howden Dams**, with their distinctive castellated twin towers, were the first to be built in the valley (between 1901 and 1916), and they were major engineering feats of the time. A work force of about 1,000 navvies were employed on the massive task, and they were housed with their families in a temporary village clad in corrugated iron at Birchinlee known as Tin Town, of which nothing now remains. A temporary railway line brought the gritstone blocks for the dam from quarries near Grindleford, lower down the valley.

After a thorough exploration of the Upper Derwent, return down the valley road and turn left at the A57 over the Ashopton Viaduct towards Sheffield. The ★ **Ladybower Inn** sits on the left before the road ascends the wooded clough to **Cutthroat Bridge**, scene of a murder in the 16th century. The road now enters open moorland and climbs to an enclosed area known as Hollow Meadows where, in the 1840s, the Duke of Norfolk attempted an ambitious programme of land reclamation on the bleak Moscar Moors. After the moors, the descent passes the conifer plantations around the Rivelin Reservoirs on the right and enters the western suburbs of Sheffield.

Ladybower Inn

Route 6

The green in Castleton

Around Castleton and the Hope Valley

Castleton – Hope – Navio – Bradwell – Peak Forest – Eldon Hole – Sparrowpit – Mam Nick – Edale – Hope – Castleton (**26 miles / 42km**) *See map on pages 14–15*

39

This short circular route takes in some of the finest limestone wonders of the Peak District as well as the scenic Hope Valley and the 'secret valley' of Edale.

Castleton is one of the major tourist honeypots of the Peak District and therefore a place to be avoided on busy summer weekends. It is no surprise that so many people want to visit this trim little township, spread out beneath the dominating 12th-century castle that gave it its name. The natural wonders of Castleton include four popular show caves displaying the unique semi-precious mineral known as Blue John, the tremendous limestone gorges of the Winnats Pass and Cave Dale, and the towering, tottering cliff of Mam Tor – 'the Shivering Mountain' – which encloses the western end of the Hope Valley.

Blue John stone goblet

The broad shale-grit Hucklow Edge runs off the Hope Valley to the south, with the village of Bradwell, which has its own caves, beneath. The whole of this area was once part of the Royal Forest of the Peak, an echo of which remains in the name of the village of Peak Forest, which also has a major pothole at Eldon Hole. Edale village, really a series of hamlets, shelters beneath the southern edge of the Peak's reigning summit, Kinder Scout.

★★★ **Castleton** is the 'capital' of the Hope Valley, and it owes its fortune to its strategic importance and its physical geography. Ever since the Celtic Brigantes tribe built their massive, dominating hillfort on the windswept

Castleton's Garland Queen

Mam Tor dominates

Peveril Castle

Garland King on horseback

1,698-ft (517-m) summit of ★★★ **Mam Tor** (National Trust) to the west of the village, this area has been the military and administrative centre of the valley.

However, the modern village only came into existence after the building of ★★★ **Peveril Castle** (English Heritage, daily May to October 10am–6pm, November to April 10am–4pm; closed for lunch 1–2pm) by William Peverel, William the Conqueror's illegitimate son, soon after the Norman Conquest. Situated on a limestone spur between the precipitous slopes of ★★ **Cave Dale** and the huge chasm of **Peak Cavern**, the castle is about as impregnable as a castle could be. Not much remains of Peverel's early structure apart from some herringbone masonry in the north curtain wall overlooking the village. The small stone keep was built in the 12th century, and the views from the ramparts are as fine as any in the Peak District, extending from Mam Tor in the northwest across the Back Tor–Lose Hill ridge to Win Hill in the northeast.

It is easy to see from the vantage point of the castle how the village was designed as an easily defended township within an encircling ★★ **Town Ditch**, best accessed by turning left as you leave the central village car park. Prominent in the centre of the village is the ★★★ **Parish Church of St Edmund**, probably originally built as a garrison church associated with the castle, as the Norman work in the chancel arch might indicate. Most of the present church dates from the extensive restoration carried out in 1837, but the lovely 17th-century box pews were spared.

The church plays an important part in Castleton's unique **Garland Ceremony**, which takes place on Oak Apple Day – 29 May each year. On their white horses, the Garland King and Queen lead a procession through the village. The King is encased from head to waist in the 'garland', a wooden cage covered in spring flowers. The procession calls at all the village pubs, where a special garland tune is played and the children dance, then ends up at the church, where the garland is strung up to the top of the church tower and left to wither. The custom is thought to have its origins in a Pagan ceremony to welcome the end of winter and the return of spring.

Most people come to Castleton to visit the famous showcaves, the oldest of which is probably ★★★ **Peak Cavern** (Easter to the end of October daily 10am–5pm, 4.30pm in low season). The entrance to Peak Cavern is said to be the largest in Britain, under a 300-ft (90-m) cliff of limestone over which towers Peveril Castle. Inside, the spacious entrance area was once the home of a community of rope-makers, whose equipment still survives. The soot from their homes in this village that never saw the sun still blackens the roof. Queen Victoria and Lord Byron were among the early visitors.

The ★★ **Speedwell Cavern** (daily 9.30am–5.30pm, 4.30pm in winter) is at the foot of the ★★★ **Winnats Pass** (National Trust) just outside the village, and it is unique because the visitor is transported to the Bottomless Pit by a boat that is legged along a flooded lead mine drainage level like a barge in a canal tunnel.

Winnats Pass

The Winnats Pass is a spectacular limestone gorge formed after the last Ice Age. The scene of a tragic murder of a pair of lovers in the 18th century, it is now the only road out of the Hope Valley to the west. The former A625 turnpike road led beneath the crumbling slopes of Mam Tor, but constant landslips from this Shivering Mountain led to its closure in the early 1970s and the reinstatement of the old Winnats Pass route.

★★★ **Treak Cliff Cavern** (March to October daily 9.30am–5.30pm, November to February 10am–4pm) probably has the most spectacular formations of Castleton's show caves, and it is one of the few sources of the semi-precious banded fluorspar known as Blue John. Ornaments made from this brilliant yet brittle mineral are sold here and in the village shops.

Treak Cliff Cavern

Blue John stone

The fourth of Castleton's show caves, the ★★ **Blue John Cavern** (daily 9.30am–6pm or dusk) is now reached by car by turning right and right again at the top of the Winnats Pass. This cavern was discovered 300 years ago when miners in search of Blue John broke into this previously unknown range of caves.

Further details of Castleton's fascinating history can be discovered by a visit to the ★★★ **Castleton Village Museum** (Easter and Bank Holiday weekends 2–5pm; May, September and October Sunday only; June and July Sunday and Wednesday; August Sunday and Tuesday to Thursday) in the Methodist Church Meeting Room to the right of the main village car park.

St Peter's Church well dressing

Navio Roman Fort

Drystone walls near Bradwell

Leave Castleton by the A625 Sheffield road. Hiding behind trees to the left is **Losehill Hall**, **the Peak National Park Study Centre**, which offers a range of courses and holidays in countryside conservation and management. After about 2 miles (3km) the road enters the village of **Hope**, whose former importance as a centre of the Royal Forest of the Peak is reflected in the fact that it, and not Castleton, gave its name to the entire valley. The squat ★★ **Parish Church of St Peter** dates mainly from the 14th century but has memorials of former Forest officials and a Saxon preaching cross in the churchyard. Hope still has a weekly livestock market serving the surrounding farms. The massive Hope Valley Cement Works, whose towering white chimney dominates the valley, is just to the south.

About a mile from Hope opposite a public house, take the right turn on the B6049 toward Bradwell. Just after crossing a narrow bridge in Brough there is limited parking to the right, and a cast metal sign by a stile announces the site of one of the most important Roman sites in the National Park. This is ★★ **Navio Roman Fort** (English Heritage), a small playing-card shaped site which, with an extensive settlement outside, was probably the central control point for Roman lead-mining interests in the area. It holds a strategic position at the junction of the River Noe and Peakshole Water on Roman roads linking Aquae Arnemetiae (Buxton) and Melandra (Glossop).

The B6049 leads into the former lead mining village of **Bradwell**, which spreads along the road beneath the escarpment of Bradwell Edge to the east. Bradwell was famous for making Bradder Beavers, the hard felt hats worn by local lead miners. ★ **Bagshawe Cavern** (daily by appointment, tel: 01433 620540), off Jeffrey Lane up the hill to the right of the main street, was discovered by lead miners and is now the setting for adventure caving trips, especially for young people.

The road winds up out of Bradwell village through the imposing crags of Bradwell Dale and past the mullioned windows of **Hazelbadge Hall** (private), built in 1549 as a yeoman's farmhouse. The gliders of the Lancashire and Derbyshire Gliding Club can often be seen soaring above the limestone pastures below Hucklow Edge, where the club has its landing field. Passing through the hamlet of **Windmill**, the road reaches the crossroads at Tideswell Lane Head, where a right turn leads onto the A623 that links Chesterfield and Chapel-en-le-Frith. The road crosses the rolling pastures of Tideswell Moor and then some sharp hairpins lead to the village of **Peak Forest**.

The 17th-century ★ **Parish Church of King Charles the Martyr** owes its unusual dedication to being founded as a private chapel by the 2nd Countess of Devonshire.

For many years, because it was outside ecclesiastical laws, it was a kind of Derbyshire Gretna Green where runaway couples got married. A lane leading off opposite the church leads to one of the fabled Wonders of the Peak, the dangerous open pothole of ★★ **Eldon Hole**. Long thought to be bottomless, explorers in the 18th century discovered that it was a finite but imposing drop of 245 ft (75m).

From Peak Forest, the road leads on to the hamlet of **Sparrowpit**, where the B6061 leads through Perryfoot and past the ugly scar of **Eldon Hill Quarry** on the right.

Turn left at the head of the Winnats Pass (or straight ahead to return to Castleton) and then left again below the brooding slopes of Mam Tor onto the A625, turning sharply right to Edale via the narrow and steep Mam Nick road, which passes between Mam Tor and Rushup Edge. This minor road drops steeply down into the Edale Valley, with magnificent views of the **Kinder Scout** plateau ahead. Turn right at **Barber Booth**, one of the five 'booths' or cattle shelters which make up Edale. After about a mile (1.5km), there is a large pay-and-display car park on the left and a minor road leads up to **Grindsbrook Booth**, usually known as Edale village, where there is a **National Park Visitor Centre** (Easter to end October daily 9am–5.30pm, November to March 9am–5pm).

Edale marks the southern terminus of the 250-mile (400-km) **Pennine Way**, which marches along Britain's backbone between the Peak and the Scottish Border. This is serious walking country, and daily weather forecasts are available at the visitor centre, which doubles up as a mountain rescue point.

From Edale, turn left (east) on the valley road that threads through the valley and back into Hope, where a right turn onto the A625 leads back to Castleton.

Edale's Old Nag's Head

43

Starting out up Kinder Scout

Route 7

The Central Plateau

Buxton – Miller's Dale – Tideswell – Foolow – Eyam – Stoney Middleton – Calver – Hassop – Ashford in the Water – Taddington – Buxton (32 miles / 51km) *See map on pages 14–15*

The Central or White Peak Plateau of the Peak District is a landscape of settlement. Rolling limestone pastures are criss-crossed by many miles of drystone-wall networks and split by steep-sided dales. In sheltered spots, ancient grey-stone villages seem to grow naturally from the rock. It is a landscape steeped in history and greatly changed by human hands over the centuries. Pastoral and mainly agricultural now, it was the scene of intense industry during the 18th and 19th centuries, when farmers doubled as lead miners. The area is dotted with old shafts and spoil heaps. Once seen as the ugly waste of industry, these are now treasured as part of the region's heritage.

Even the dales did not escape the Industrial Revolution, as the former cotton mills at Litton and Cressbrook show, and villages like Tideswell, with its magnificent church, Ashford, Eyam and Stoney Middleton all show evidence of their industrial past. But peace has returned to many of the dales now, and several form part of the Derbyshire Dales National Nature Reserve – a haven for limestone-loving plants and many birds and animals.

Leave **Buxton** *(see page 25)* by the A6 east towards Bakewell, passing through the wooded confines of Ashwood Dale, through which the River Wye on the left has cut a fine gorge. When the trees give way to open pastures,

Foolow village pond

Tideswell: St John the Baptist

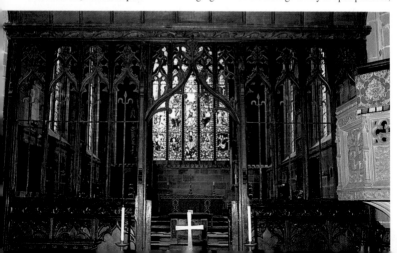

the ugly scar of **Topley Pike Quarry** is passed on the right.

At the top of the next hill, a large layby on the left reveals the huge rockface of **Tunstead Quarry**, one of the largest in Europe. These enormous limestone quarries around Buxton meant the spa town was excluded when the Peak District National Park was designated in 1951.

The A6 soon reaches the top of the limestone plateau, and at the next road junction, turn left on the B6049, dropping down by a steep hairpin into the valley of the Wye at ★★ **Miller's Dale**. The former station here (there is a pay-and-display car park) was once an important terminus on the Midland Line, for it provided the only rail access to the burgeoning spa town of Buxton, reached on a branch line from here.

Miller's Dale cafe

Today the station is a briefing centre for rangers on the ★★ **Monsal Trail**, a popular walking and riding route which follows the line of the former Midland Railway between Bakewell and the eastern outskirts of Buxton. The line was converted to a trail when the National Park authority purchased it in 1980.

A short walk westwards from Miller's Dale Station brings the visitor to the magnificent limestone buttresses of Chee Tor, site of some of the most severe rock climbs in the Peak, where the former railway line enters a now-closed tunnel. The Monsal Trail follows the river into the lovely tree-lined Chee Dale.

45

Return to the car park and turn left on leaving to climb out of the dale on the steep road that leads east and then north on the daleside towards **Tideswell**, one of the largest and most important of the Peak District villages. Its wealth was founded on the traditional dual economies of sheep rearing and lead mining. The superb ★★★ **Parish Church of St John the Baptist**, watching over the Pot Market, is the most complete medieval church in the Peak and is known, with some justification, as the Cathedral of the Peak. It was built, unusually for English churches, in about 50 years from around 1320, and it illustrates the transition between the late Decorated style, as shown in the light and airy chancel, and the later Perpendicular style, illustrated to elegant effect in the tall, pinnacled west tower, a landmark for miles around.

Tideswell: well dressing design and surrounding countryside

The builder of this splendid church was probably Sir John Foljambe, of a prominent local landowning family, whose 14th-century brass is in the sanctuary. Among a number of other outstanding brasses, the splendid 16th-century example of Bishop Robert Pursglove is in the chancel. This Tideswell man founded the ancient Grammar School nearby and changed from being a Protestant bishop under Edward VI to a Roman Catholic bishop under Mary Tudor. Note also the vigorous carving in the choir

Carving in the church

stalls and the north transept screen, guarding the chapel of the craft Guild of St Mary, all of which are by the local Hunstone family.

★★ **The George Inn**, to the east of the church, is noted for its fine Venetian-style windows, dating from the late 18th century. Tideswell was granted its charter for a weekly market and fair as early as 1251, a reflection of its importance as one of the principal courts of the Royal Forest of the Peak. The village's well-dressings, held during the Wakes week at the end of June, are among the finest in the Peak.

Foolow: ducks and surroundings

Leave Tideswell by the B6049 north, crossing the A623 at Tideswell Lane Ends, and turn right on the minor road that crosses the dry valley of Silly Dale to enter the village of **Foolow**, a humorous combination for many. Foolow clusters around its village green and circular duckpond (the 'mere'), and there is evidence of the once-extensive lead mining in the fields all around.

Continue on this road eastwards under the escarpment of Hucklow Edge to the left. The 17th-century hostelry of the Barrel Inn at Bretton – one of the oldest and most characterful inns in the Peak District – is prominent on the skyline. Fluorspar is now mined under this escarpment at the Ladywash Mine.

The road leads down into the famous plague village of **Eyam** (pronounced 'Eem'), beneath wooded Eyam Edge. This was the scene, in the mid-17th century, of what has been described as 'one of the epic stories in the annals of rural life.' The Great (or more accurately Bubonic) Plague came to Eyam in 1665, apparently in a bundle of flea-ridden cloth from London. It quickly spread through the tiny village, eventually killing something between a quarter and a third of the population.

Led by their rector, the Reverend William Mompesson, and his non-conformist predecessor, Thomas Stanley, the villagers resolved to impose a quarantine on their own movements – they erected a *cordon sanitaire* around the village so that the deadly infection would not spread further. In another attempt to control the spread of the disease, the ★★★ **Parish Church of St Lawrence** (which has some interesting Plague memorials) was abandoned and services were held in the natural amphitheatre known as Cucklett Delf, just to the south of the village. Every year a commemorative service is held at Cucklett Delf, combined with the village well-dressings.

Memories of the tragic Plague days are everywhere in and around the busy little village. Individual cottages carry plaques showing who died there three centuries ago, including the **Plague Cottage** (private), next to the church, where the Plague arrived. As the disease spread unchecked

Eyam: Plague Cottage

within the village, about 260 people are thought to have died, including Katherine Mompesson, the rector's wife, whose tabletop grave is in the churchyard.

Plague memorial

To avoid infection, whole families were buried in the fields around the village in places such as the ★★ **Riley Graves** (National Trust) about half a mile (0.8km) east of the village centre. Elsewhere on the outskirts of the village, food and supplies were left for the villagers by grateful outsiders. The Plague story is well told in the ★★★ **Eyam Museum** in Hawkshill Road (March to November Tuesday to Sunday 10am–4.30pm, closed Monday except Bank Holidays).

Opposite the small village green, complete with stocks no longer in use, is the romantic 17th-century manor house of ★★★ **Eyam Hall** (Wednesday, Thursday, the weekend and Bank Holiday Mondays, end of March to November, 11am–4pm), which has been in the Wright family since it was built three centuries ago and was partly opened to the public only recently. Don't miss the Jacobean staircase and the wonderful early tapestries in the bedrooms. The house includes a Buttery and gift shop plus a newly opened ★ **Craft Centre** (March to December daily except Monday 10.30am–5pm).

Eyam Hall

Leave Eyam by turning right just past the church, taking a road that leads steeply down Eyam Dale to the junction with the A632. Turn left onto this busy road, which leads east into the confines of Middleton Dale. High natural crags to the left and dusty quarry workings to the right prelude entry into the village of **Stoney Middleton**.

'Stoney', as it is usually known, suffers somewhat from the heavy traffic passing through, but at the village centre the left turn in front of the **Toll House** (built in 1840 and later converted into a fish and chip shop) leads to the quiet backwater known as The Nook. Here, on Blind Lane, stands the odd building known as the ★ **Roman Baths** but actually built in 1815 by Lord Denman, Chief Justice of England, who lived at Stoney Middleton Hall. The recently-restored Bath House is fed by thermal springs, which may well have originally attracted the Romans, like those at Buxton. The ★★ **Parish Church of St Martin's** is one of the most unusual in the Peak District, with a spacious octagonal 18th-century nave tacked on to a 15th-century Perpendicular tower.

Stoney Middleton: St Martin's Church interior

Continue east on the A623 to the traffic lights and crossroads at **Calver Sough** (a sough is a drainage tunnel from a lead mine). Turn right on the B6001 towards Bakewell and after about a mile (1.5km), you reach the hamlet of **Hassop**, with another unusual church in the shape of the Doric temple, classical-revival style Roman Catholic

Hassop Hall and Monsal Dale

Ashford: painting the Sheepwash Bridge

Church of All Saints, which dates from 1816. The Roman Catholic denomination of the church reflects the religious beliefs of the Eyre family, which since the Middle Ages has held nearby **Hassop Hall** (private), a mainly Jacobean mansion and now one of the best hotels and restaurants in the Peak District.

Go past the church and turn right on the minor road just in front of the entrance gates to Hassop Hall. This leads to the village of **Great Longstone**, with its rare 18th-century brick-built hall (private) on the right, and then **Little Longstone**, with its tiny Packhorse Inn.

The road winds up to ★★★ **Monsal Head**, one of the most popular and photographed viewpoints in the Peak District. A convenient car park affords a sweeping view down into the valley of the Wye as it winds between limestone hills like **Fin Cop** (1,073ft / 327m, and the site of an Iron Age hillfort – no access) and Putwell Hill. Dwarfed in the valley below is the ★★ **Monsal Dale Viaduct**, built to carry the Midland Line and now part of the **Monsal Trail**. The viaduct can be easily reached by taking a steep path down through the trees.

Turn left at the road junction from Little Longstone onto the B6465, which leads down to the pretty village of **Ashford in the Water**. The 'water' is the River Wye, and one of Ashford's attractions is the 17th-century ★★ **Sheepwash Bridge**. The bridge is closed to traffic, but it is still occasionally used for its original purpose of washing sheep – which are corralled in the integral pen.

Ashford's ★★ **Parish Church of Holy Trinity** was heavily restored in 1870, but it has a rare tympanum over a Norman doorway. The squat tower may date from the 13th century, but most of the rest is a century later. The church has tablet memorials made from what is called Ashford Black Marble, but which is in reality a highly polished grey limestone mined locally. This marble became very fashionable in Victorian times.

Reaching the A6 at Ashford, turn right (west) towards Buxton, passing through the lovely Wye Valley before climbing through the trees of Ashwood Dale and out onto the plateau. The village of **Taddington** lies to the left where the road becomes a dual carriageway.

Cut into the limestone hills just to the west of Taddington is one of the highest Neolithic chambered tombs in the country at ★★ **Five Wells** (English Heritage). The chamber is reached by a bridleway leading up from the Waterloo Hotel, and the site commands wonderful views across the Wye Valley.

Within a mile (1.5km) on the A6, the Miller's Dale turn is reached again, but continue straight ahead and back into Buxton by the outward route.

Route 8

The Derwent and Wye Valleys

Bakewell – Baslow – Chatsworth – Beeley – Rowsley – Haddon Hall – Bakewell (13 miles/21km) *See map on pages 14–15*

Bakewell Carnival

This short circular route takes in two of the most famous and popular stately homes in the Peak District – Chatsworth and Haddon Hall. A full day will be needed to explore them both properly.

The route starts and ends in Bakewell, the 'capital' of the Peak District. The busy little market town on the River Wye has been an important commercial centre for over 1,000 years. Bakewell's market charter dates from 1254, but the original settlement is much older. Monday has been market day for at least 700 years, and local farmers from throughout the Peak District gather to buy and sell their stock in the biggest livestock exchange in the area. Ironically, Bakewell's greatest claim to fame began life as an accident in the kitchens of the Rutland Arms Hotel in the centre of town – it is a dessert known locally as a Bakewell pudding, *never* a Bakewell tart.

Enjoy some Bakewell pudding

Although **Bakewell's** population is only 4,000, its fine warm gritstone buildings and commercial situation make it feel like a town, and it is usually known as such. It owes its existence to the crossing of the Wye now accomplished by one of the finest 14th-century bridges still in use in the country. Just across the bridge is the tree-topped mound long thought to be the 9th-century 'burh' created by Alfred's son, Edward the Elder, to receive the homage of the warring kingdoms of the rest of England, and thus arguably become the first king of Britain. How-

Church of All Saints: Saxon cross

In the Old House Museum

Puddings for sale

ever, excavations have revealed the mound to be a motte dating from the troubled times of the late 12th century, and Edward's 'burh' has still to be conclusively identified.

But there is no doubt that Bakewell's history extends to Saxon times. A visit to the ★★★ **Parish Church of All Saints** reveals a wealth of Saxon material, including two of the finest Saxon preaching crosses in the Peak District in the churchyard. Heavily restored in Victorian times, the cruciform church still has fragments of Saxon and Norman work, although the elegant spire standing on its octagonal tower dates from the 19th-century rebuilding. Inside the church there are a number of fine monuments, notably in the Vernon Chapel. Here a rather stern looking Dorothy Vernon of Haddon Hall fame kneels facing her husband John Manners, the controversial coupling which linked two of the most powerful local families. There is also an earlier monument to Sir George Vernon, 'the King of the Peak'. The south porch is filled with an amazing collection of Saxon carved stones, indicating that the *coenubium* or monastery mentioned in a charter of AD949 may have housed a school of craftsmen who sculpted the crosses here and at Eyam.

Just behind the church in Cunningham Place is the fascinating ★★★ **Old House Museum** (April to the end of October daily 2–5pm), one of the finest local museums in the country. It is housed in a Tudor house of 1534, which was later used for workers employed by Richard Arkwright who had a mill (now demolished) on the Wye at Bakewell. There are collections of local memorabilia, costumes, lace, samplers and toys, and the Victorian kitchen is retained, along with other recreated craftsmen's workshops, by the local historical society.

Back in the centre of town, the ★★ **Old Market Hall National Park and Tourist Information Centre** (Easter to October 9.30am–5.30pm, 6pm weekends and Bank Holidays; winter 9.30am–5pm, Thursday 9am–1pm) in Bridge Street is worth a visit. The building dates from the 17th century, and it was an open, arcaded market hall before its conversion first to shops and then a library and information centre. Displays tell the story of the town and the Peak District, and regular audio-visual shows and talks are presented upstairs in the half-timbered roof space. There is a well-stocked shop area where maps and guides to the district can be obtained.

Outside the visitor centre is the bow-fronted ★★ **Old Original Bakewell Pudding Shop**, one of three in the town that claim to hold the original recipe to this almond and puff pastry delicacy. The story is that it was created when a flustered cook at the 17th-century Rutland Arms Hotel in nearby Rutland Square poured her pastry mix over the jam instead of the other way around.

Leave Bakewell by the A619 Baslow (Chesterfield) road over the magnificent bridge, passing the headquarters of the National Park on the left as the road climbs out of Bakewell. Follow the A619 to the outskirts of **Baslow**, which is worth a visit if only to admire the broached spire of the 13th–14th century ★★ **Parish Church**, whose clock tower displays the name VICTORIA 1897 instead of numbers on the clock face in commemoration of Queen Victoria's jubilee. Baslow also has some fine bridges: one has a diminutive tollhouse at one end and another, at Nether End, is watched over by one of the few thatched cottages in the Peak District.

To cut Baslow from the route, turn right at the junction of the A619 and the B6012 outside the village and follow the Derwent valley into the grounds of Chatsworth. As you cross the cattle grid to enter the parklands, a road to the right leads into the model village of **Edensor** (pronounced Ensor), created by the 6th Duke of Devonshire in 1842 when the original village was transplanted to the present site. The elegant spire of the parish church was designed by Sir George Gilbert Scott, and the churchyard contains the graves of several members of the Cavendish family as well as Kathleen Kennedy, sister of the American President John F. Kennedy, who was married to the Marquis of Hartington.

Church in the model village of Edensor

51

Home of the Dukes of Devonshire for some 400 years, ★★★ **Chatsworth House** (end of March to November daily 11am–4.30pm, gardens June to August 11am–5pm) is one of the finest houses in England and known as 'the Palace of the Peak'. A veritable treasure house of works of art which have been collected over the years by successive dukes, the house has been described by the present Duchess as 'not so much a house as a town'.

Chatsworth House

Highlights of the tour of the house include the magnificent and recently cleaned ★★ **Painted Hall** by Louis Laguerre, which shows sumptuous scenes from the life of Julius Caesar. This grand hall is the scene every year of the Chatsworth children's Christmas Party, and other grand functions. The ★★ **State Rooms**, including the **Dining Room**, **Drawing Room**, **Music Room** (note Jan Vandervaart's famous *trompe l'oeil* violin 'hanging' behind a door) and **Dressing Room and Bedroom** are simply stunning in their opulence. Note particularly the superb 17th-century English tapestries in the Drawing Room and the wonderful painted ceiling, again by Laguerre, showing Dawn chasing away Night, in the State Bedroom.

The waterfall

The many family portraits displayed in the ★★ **Sketch Galleries** show the Duke's continuing interest in art, while the ★★ **Sculpture Gallery** illustrates the 6th Duke's particular passion. It includes the famous Chatsworth *tazza*,

Chatsworth gardens

Life on the Children's Farm

the biggest piece made from Blue John. The ★★ **Great Dining Room** is where the young Princess Victoria had her first dinner with the grown-ups in 1832. It has recently been redecorated in lovely ruby silk panelling, and is notable for its its gold-encrusted barrel ceiling and fine collection of paintings.

On a different scale, but in its own way just as impressive, is the series of small rooms known as the ★★ **Queen of Scots Rooms**, where that unfortunate monarch lodged in the old house during several stays between 1570 and 1581.

The house as we see it today is largely the creation of the 4th Earl and the Dutch architect William Talman, and it was built in the Palladian style between 1678 and 1707. The only part of Bess of Hardwick's Tudor house that is left is the ★★ **Hunting Tower** (private), up through the trees of Stand Wood behind the house. Also in Stand Wood is the ★★ **Chatsworth Children's Farm and Adventure Playground** (end of March to end of September daily 10.30am–4.30pm) where children can see (and touch) farm animals and watch regular milking demonstrations.

Leave Chatsworth by the B6012, which winds through superb deer-stocked parklands created by 'Capability' Brown for the 4th Duke in the 1760s, to reach the estate village of **Beeley**. Beeley has a fine 17th-century Old Hall (private) and one of several pubs in this locality with the tell-tale name of The Devonshire Arms. From Beeley continue on to **Rowsley**, where the Midland Railway terminated until 1863 in a fine station designed by Joseph Paxton, the architect of so much of the Chatsworth estate. Turn right here on the A6 towards Bakewell.

Rowsley is really a Haddon village, not a Chatsworth village, as illustrated by the fine peacock crest over the door of the splendid **Peacock Hotel** in the centre of the village. Built in 1652 as a private house, it became an inn in 1828 and is now the epitome of an English country inn. Opposite the Peacock, a side road leads across a bridge to ★★★ **Caudwell's Mill and Craft Centre** (March to October daily 10am–6pm, November to February weekends only 10am–4.30pm). This 19th-century mill on the Wye is one of few working water-powered roller mills. It was lovingly restored by a group of enthusiasts and still produces flour for sale. The former stableyard is the centre of a 'village' of local craftspeople.

Caudwell's Craft Centre

About a mile from Rowsley on the A6 is the second of the Peak's most famous stately homes. Hiding modestly behind a tall beech hedge is ★★★ **Haddon Hall** (April to end of September daily 11am–5.45pm, closed on Sunday in July and August), home of the Duke of Rutland and often described as 'the most romantic medieval manor house in England.' It is a description which is hard to argue with as you approach the turreted north-west tower standing proudly on its limestone bluff above the narrow 17th-century bridge across the Wye.

Haddon Hall

53

If certain scenes in Haddon provoke recognition, it should be no surprise. Such is its medieval perfection, it has served as the location for many television and cinema films. Strangely, Haddon is remarkably complete in appearance because the family virtually abandoned the house in the 18th and 19th centuries, preferring Belvoir Castle. This meant there were no constant 'improvements' as happened at neighbouring Chatsworth, and most of what you see from the sloping ★★ **Lower Courtyard** dates from the 14th and 15th centuries.

Haddon's time-worn steps and oak-panelled rooms breathe history. Among the highlights are the wonderful ★★ **Banqueting Hall**, the very essence of a medieval manor house complete with minstrels gallery and massive 13th-century oak refectory table. The ★★ **Long Gallery**, with elaborate oak panelling featuring the boar's head of the Vernons and the peacock of the Manners, is wonderfully light and airy and has some very good diamond-paned glass. Many people's favourite area is, however, the ★★ **Kitchen**, stone-flagged and walled with massive oak tables, chopping blocks and mixing bowls almost worn through with centuries of use. The larder includes a fine collection of dole cupboards.

The Long Gallery

The ★★ **Chapel of St Nicholas** is one of the oldest parts of the house, and it originally served the now-disappeared village of Nether Haddon. It contains some of the finest 14th- and 15th-century wall paintings in Britain. The tour ends with the famous terraced gardens: a riot of roses, clematis and other blossoms in summer.

Route 9

Matlock, Ashbourne and Dove Dale

Matlock – Matlock Bath – Cromford – Wirksworth – Carsington – Ashbourne – Dove Dale – Ilam – Alstonefield – Hartington – Matlock (42 miles / 68km)

The 17th-century traveller Daniel Defoe described the River Derwent as 'that fury of a river'. But a century later the first true industrialists like Richard Arkwright recognised that if the 'fury' could be harnessed, they would have the most vital ingredient for industry – power.

That is why Arkwright, one of the architects of the Industrial Revolution, came to Cromford in 1771 to build the world's first water-powered cotton mill and create an industrial village that was a wonder of the age. Better communications might have made the Derwent Valley at Cromford and Matlock one of the principal centres of that world-shattering revolution. Industry was in the valley already in the numerous lead mines, the remains of which still scatter the southern limestone plateau. But thanks to Izaak Walton and Charles Cotton, Dove Dale, just north of the market town of Ashbourne, was attracting the first of the tourists that now make the southern Peak District one of the busiest parts of the park, especially in summer.

Matlock: view of Riber Castle

It is appropriate that **Matlock** is the administrative centre of Derbyshire, for its Old English name means 'oak where a moot was held'. The offices of Derbyshire County Council overlook the bustling little town, since 1958 occupying John Smedley's former hydropathic hotel and health establishment, built in 1853 to answer the popular demand for spa cures. Visitors reached the 'Hydro' by taking a tram up the steep hill from the town centre.

Smedley created the modern Matlock, watching over its development from the fairy-tale mock-Gothic and now ruined folly of **Riber Castle**, which overlooks the town from its commanding hilltop to the south. The castle is now the centre of the ★★ **Riber Wildlife Park** (daily from 10am). Riber specialises in European birds and animals, and it runs an important breeding programme for European lynx and other rare and endangered species.

Riber Wildlife Park

Leave Matlock by the A6 south towards Derby, taking the bridge over the Derwent and passing almost immediately into the Derwent Gorge, where high limestone crags crowd in on the left. Soon the biggest of the lot, the 300-ft (90-m) **High Tor** appears almost overhanging the road. Sometimes, rock climbers can be seen clinging to the tremendous rockface like flies on a wall.

Just beyond High Tor, the swinging gondolas of the ★★ **Heights of Abraham Cable Cars** (daily 10am–4.30pm, February–March weekends only) will be seen across the gorge ahead. The Heights of Abraham, named after Wolfe's famous victory in Quebec in 1759 and reached by turning left as you enter **Matlock Bath**, also includes the ★★ **Rutland and Great Masson Show Caverns** (same times as above), both former lead mines that now provide exciting underground tours, picnic sites and nature trails up to the **Victoria Prospect Tower**, built in 1844 and commanding stupendous views across the gorge.

Ascending the Heights of Abraham

Close to the terminus of the cable cars is the Swiss-cottage style former Matlock Bath station, now the Derbyshire Wildlife Trust's ★★ **Whistlestop Countryside Centre** (daily 10am–5pm, November to March weekends only), which displays aspects of the county's wildlife.

Matlock Bath became popular as a holiday destination in Victorian times when the railway came and the Derby road was created from Cromford. Today, it is well-known as a weekend destination for bikers and for its autumn illuminations over the Lover's Walks along the Derwent.

Among its modern attractions is the ★★★ **Peak District Mining Museum** (daily 11am–4pm) in the Pavilion. This offers a fascinating introduction to the world of the lead miner, with tunnels through which children can crawl.

Matlock Bath: Jubilee Bridge

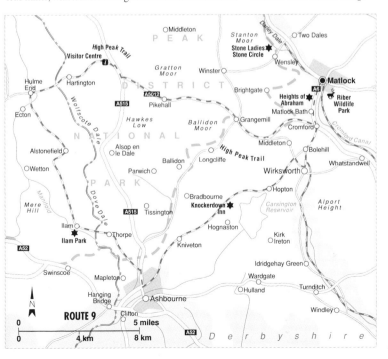

★ **Gulliver's Kingdom Theme Park** (Easter to end of September daily 10.30am–5pm, October weekends only) is set high on a hillside above Matlock Bath to the west.

Follow the A6 through Matlock Bath past the New Bath Hotel (1735) on the right and the red brick **Masson Mill** on the left (private) on the site of Richard Arkwright's Derwent-powered cotton mill of 1784. The road now enters Arkwright's planned township of **Cromford**, which he came to in 1771 to build the world's first water-powered cotton mill. That building is now the ★★ **Arkwright Mill** (Monday to Friday 9am–5pm), an international heritage site with a range of gift shops, reached by turning left at the Scarthin Nick traffic lights. A little further on down this road is Cromford Wharf and the ★ **High Peak Junction Workshops** (Easter to September 10.30am–5pm, winter weekends 10.30am–4.30pm) of the ★★ **Cromford Canal**, which runs for 5 miles (8km) to Ambergate.

High Peak Junction Workshops

Cromford Canal

56

Tours are arranged from the Arkwright Mill around the village, the main part of which is on the other side of the A6. The **Greyhound Hotel** (1778) and Arkwright's workers' cottages, in North Street off the Wirksworth road, which were completed in 1776, show how the new industrialist wanted to look after his workers.

Turn right at the Scarthin Nick crossroads and then left on the B5036 up a steep hill, passing on the left the outstanding viewpoint of the crags of the ★★ **Black Rocks of Cromford**. Here there is a picnic site and access to the ★★ **High Peak Trail**, a leisure route that follows the line of the former Cromford and High Peak Railway, completed in 1831 as an extension of the Cromford Canal.

As the road enters quarry-scarred Wirksworth, signs indicate the ★★★ **National Stone Centre** (March to October daily 10am–5pm, October to March 10am–4pm)

Black Rocks of Cromford

in Porter Lane, an exciting new visitor attraction that tells the varied story of stone through treasure trails, audio-visual shows and exhibitions, all contained in a former limestone quarry by the High Peak Trail.

Wirksworth has been a centre for lead mining for centuries, a story graphically told in the ★★ **Wirksworth Heritage Centre** (February 10 to March 29 and October 30 to December 1, Wednesday to Saturday 11am–4pm, Sunday from 1pm; March 30 to July 26 and September 10 to October 27, Tuesday to Saturday and Bank Holidays, 10.30am–4.30pm, Sunday from 1–4.30pm; July 27 to September 8, daily 10am–5pm). Created in a former silk and velvet mill, this award-winning centre has three floors of interpretive displays and exhibits, including a replica quarryman's house from the early 1900s.

Wirksworth Heritage Centre: famous locals

Wirksworth's sloping **Market Place** has many fine 18th- and 19th-century buildings, and the ★★ **Moot Hall** (not open to the public) is the scene of the twice-yearly Barmote Court, which still administers the ancient laws of the lead miners. Inside is kept the brass standard measuring dish (it holds 14 pints of ore) given to the court by Henry VIII in 1512. The ★★ **Parish Church of St Mary** is mainly 13th-century, and contains a wonderful carved coffin lid from the 7th century. Tucked away in the wall of the south transept is a tiny carving of a lead miner, brought here from Bonsall.

Moot Hall plaque

57

7th-century carved coffin lid

Leave Wirksworth by the B5035 toward Ashbourne, passing the village of **Hopton** on the right, famous for its fossil-rich limestone quarries. After about a mile (1.5km) the road passes the Knockerdown Inn on the right, which stands opposite the entrance to ★★ **Carsington Reservoir** (daily all year from 10am, closing times vary), which has flooded the shallow valley of the Scow Brook. This is the latest of the Peak District's reservoirs. Opened in 1992, it has a range of public amenities from a visitor centre, shops and restaurant to nature trails, water sports and a cycle-hire centre. The centre also recently won the 'Loo of the Year' award.

Three miles (5km) further on is the lovely Georgian market town of **Ashbourne**, which proudly announces itself as the gateway to Dove Dale. But there is much more to Ashbourne than that, as a stroll down Church Street and St John Street will show. The ★★★ **Parish Church of St Oswald** is one of the finest in the Peak District, and its soaring 14th-century spire is an elegant landmark. George Eliot thought it 'the finest mere parish church in the country', and it certainly has a cathedral-like air. Dating mainly from the 13th and 14th centuries, it is famous for its chapels in each transept and a magnificent series of monuments, notably those to the local families of the

St Oswald's Church interior

Ashbourne: a unique double

Gingerbread Shop

Ilam: Gothic-style houses
and the hall

Cokaynes and Bradbournes. There is a touching white marble sleeping figure of five-year-old Penelope Brook by Thomas Banks, dated 1793. Near the church in Church Street is the beautiful gabled and mullioned Elizabethan **Old Grammar School** of 1585 (private). On the way to Ashbourne's cobbled and sloping **Market Place**, you pass under the unique dual sign across the street of the Green Man and Black's Head hotels and by the **Ashbourne Gingerbread Shop**, which still makes the local delicacy in a restored timber-framed house. Ashbourne's ★★**Tourist Information Centre** (summer daily 9.30am–5pm, winter 10am–4pm closed Sunday) is in the Market Place.

Take the A515 Buxton Road up a steep hill north from Ashbourne. Turn left after about a mile (1.5km) on a minor road signposted to Thorpe and Dove Dale. **Thorpe** is an unpretentious limestone village standing at the foot of the eponymous Thorpe Cloud (942ft/287m), one of the sentinels of Dove Dale. ★★★ **Dove Dale** (National Trust, car park), reached by a minor road on the right through Thorpe, is probably the most famous and certainly the most popular and overused of the White Peak dales. More than a million people visit it every year, and the National Park and footpath authorities runs a continuous programme of repairs to the 7-mile (11-km) footpath that runs north through the dale to Hartington.

Many people do not go far beyond the famous **Stepping Stones** beneath Thorpe Cloud and Bunster Hill, and they miss the famous series of rock pinnacles and caves such as Tissington Spires, Ilam Rock, Pickering Tor and Reynard's Cave, with its natural archway. Dove Dale is beautiful, but it can be oppressively crowded on a summer weekend. The dale can be even lovelier in winter, when there are far fewer people.

Just beyond the Dove Dale turn is the quaint estate village of **Ilam**, largely rebuilt by the shipping magnate Jesse Watts Russell in the *cottage ornée* Gothic style around an Eleanor-type cross erected in memory of his wife. Russell lived at mock-Gothic **Ilam Hall** (National Trust, grounds and country park open all year, hall closed to the public). In the grounds stands the beautiful saddleback-towered ★★ **Church of the Holy Cross**, a mixture of Saxon, Norman and Early English styles. It is unfortunately dominated by Francis Chantrey's massive monument to Russell's father-in-law, David Pike Watts. Luckily, the ★★ **Chapel of St Bertram**, a little-known Saxon saint, was left undisturbed, as were the series of Saxon cross shafts that can be seen in the churchyard.

Take the minor road leading north across the limestone pastures between the rivers Dove (east) and Manifold (west), turning right at Hope to the pretty village of **Alstonefield**, at whose heart is the village green, watched over by the George Inn.

From Alstonefield, the lanes lead north to **Hulme End**, once a station on the Leek and Manifold Light Railway (1904–34), now a car park and cycle-hire centre on the popular **Manifold Track**. Turn right at Hulme End onto the B5054 to cross the Dove and enter **Hartington**, a once-important market town that still has a broad Market Square and important houses like the Jacobean **Hartington Hall**, once a lodging for Bonnie Prince Charlie and now a splendid youth hostel. Hartington is most famous for its **Stilton Cheese Factory**, one of only a handful in the country. The ★★ **Parish Church of St Giles** is mainly 13th-century.

Hartington, a home of Stilton cheese

Go east on the B5054 up Hand Dale to cross the line of the **Tissington Trail** at the ★★ **Hartington Station National Park Visitor Centre** (Easter to end of September weekends and Bank Holidays 10.30am–5pm, times vary), which is housed in an old railway signal box. Children are delighted to find they can operate the levers.

On reaching the A515 turn right towards Ashbourne, then turn left after about a mile (1.5km) onto the A5012 towards Cromford at **Newhaven**, opposite the sadly neglected 18th-century Newhaven Inn. This road crosses the broad limestone plateau of Elton Common and passes Grangemill and its quarries before entering the tree-clad gorge of the **Via Gellia**. The Via Gellia is not Roman, as the name might suggest, but an affectation of Philip Gell of Hopton, who built the road around 1800 to link his lead mines at Carsington to the Cromford Canal.

The road winds pleasantly down into Cromford Market Place, at which point a left turn onto the A6 will lead back to Matlock Bath and then Matlock.

Alstonefield cottage garden

The Historic Landscape

The dawn of history

Few places in Britain have as rich a variety of historic landscapes as the Peak District. Countless generations of people from the dawn of civilisation have left reminders of their presence in almost every corner.

As the glaciers of the ice age finally retreated about 10,000BC, Man gradually travelled north to explore the virgin wilderness. Traces of Paleolithic (Old Stone Age) man have been discovered in the form of rough flint blades and worked bones in caves and rock shelters in parts of the White Peak, such as the Lathkill, Dove and Manifold valleys. Thor's Cave, its entrance high in a crag overlooking the River Manifold, is the archetypal caveman's dwelling. Mesolithic (Middle Stone Age) hunter-gatherers came later on summer hunting trips into the then lightly-wooded uplands in search of game. They led a mainly nomadic existence.

Bear in Buxton Museum

The first farmers came with the dawn of the Neolithic (New Stone Age) period around 3,000BC. Animals were domesticated for the first time, and these people left behind the first recognisable monuments in the landscape. Chief among these is the magnificent henge and stone circle of Arbor Low, near Youlgreave. Archaeologists have argued for years about whether the limestone slabs of this ancient site ever stood upright, like those in their southern contemporaries at Stonehenge and Avebury, and no one can be sure about how this enigmatic site was used. There is no such mystery about the Five Wells chambered tomb at Taddington, or the Minninglow tombs above the High Peak Trail. This is where the bones of Neolithic tribal leaders were buried, watching over their ancestors below. The tradition of burying important people on the highest points in the landscape was carried on into the Bronze Age (3500–1000BC). More than 500 placenames in upland Derbyshire retain the element 'low' – Old English for a burial mound or barrow – and most of these date from the Bronze Age. Stanton Moor, a small heather-clad gritstone plateau near Bakewell, is is peppered with over 70 barrows, stone circles and standing stones. Hut circles, field systems and burial cairns have also been identified on the eastern moors above the River Derwent.

61

Bronze-Age mound at Arbor Low

The best evidence of the Iron Age in the Peak District is the system of hill forts on prominent hills, such as Mam Tor above Castleton. Despite their name, hill forts were often not purely defensive in nature but used as summer sheilings by tribespeople who probably retreated to settlements in the valleys in the winter. There are also hill forts at Castle Naze near Buxton, Fin Cop above Monsal Dale, and Carl Wark above Hathersage.

A landscape farmed for millennia

Romans and Saxons

Roman pigs of lead

The Romans came into the Peak, probably in search of lead, around AD70. Roman pigs of lead bearing the name 'Lutudarum', the undiscovered Roman lead-mining centre in the Peak District, have been found as far away as Sussex. Other attractions were the warm springs at Buxton, which the Romans named *Aquae Arnemetiae*.

The best-known Roman fort is Navio, at Brough near Hope, where a garrison of 500 men was stationed in the late 1st century. Another, larger fort existed at Melandra outside Glossop, guarding the Doctor's Gate route to Navio across the Snake Pass. Other recognised Roman roads include the present A515 between Ashbourne and Buxton, and Batham Gate across Bradwell Moor, which linked Navio with Buxton. Some Peak District valleys, especially in the White Peak, supported a far greater population in Roman times than they do now. A good example is Roystone Grange, near Ballidon just north of Ashbourne, where a thriving Romano-British farming community existed during the 2nd and 3rd centuries AD.

Roman shrine, Buxton Museum

When the Roman legions left around 410AD, Britain was plunged into a period of political and religious turmoil that used to be called the Dark Ages. In the Peak District, however, the wealth of early Saxon remains shows a well-settled and culturally active population, exemplified by the wonderful collection of Saxon carved preaching crosses, such as those found in the churchyards at Bakewell, Ilam, Eyam and Hope. Such Dark Age art is not matched in Britain south of Northumbria.

The feudal overlay

Saxon helmet, Sheffield City Museum

The mailed fist of the Norman Conquest is best illustrated in the Peak District by the commanding stone walls of Peveril Castle, which overlook the Norman township of Castleton. Little remains of that first castle, built by William the Conqueror so that his illegitimate son, William Peverel, could command the Royal Hunting Forest of the Peak. But the keep, built in the late 12th century by Henry II, remains one of the earliest stone-built keeps in the country and the Peak's finest medieval landmark. The *Domesday Book* (1086) also records a substantial settlement at Bakewell. Much of the rest of the Peak District was laid waste by William in his infamous 'harrying of the north'.

The Royal Forest of the Peak continued to attract royalty, with Edward I being a particularly frequent visitor. It was Edward who ordered the laying down of laws to cover the administration and prosecution of lead mining laws in a document known as *Quo Warranto*, set out in an inquisition held at Ashbourne in 1288. These laws are some of the earliest in the English language and are still in operation today.

Many of the great landowning families in the Peak District, such as the Eyres, the Manners, the Vernons and the Leghs, owe their extensive estates to their Feudal ancestry. The first great houses at Haddon, Chatsworth and Hardwick were built at this time, to be replaced later by the grander mansions so popular with visitors today. Much of the money for this rebuilding, and for the fine village churches of the Peak District such as Tideswell's splendid Perpendicular 'Cathedral of the Peak', came from the dual economies of lead and wool. British wool was in great demand on the Continent, and lead mining was growing in importance with the great medieval building boom.

The industrial heritage

Water power from the fast-flowing Peak District rivers was first harnessed in small corn mills, a rare working example of which still exists at Caudwells Mill, at Rowsley on the Wye. But the first water-powered cotton mill – which could arguably be said to have started the Industrial Revolution – was built by Richard Arkwright at Cromford, on the River Derwent just south of Matlock, in 1771. He was later to build further mills at Bakewell and Cressbrook on the River Wye and develop Cromford as one of the first purpose-built industrial villages.

Richard Arkwright

63

The surrounding towns of Manchester (famous for cotton mills) and Sheffield (famous for its steel forges) expanded rapidly as the Industrial Revolution took off. Other towns in the surrounding lowlands had their own specialities. The first silk mill was built in Macclesfield in 1742, and Glossop's fame as a cotton town was guaranteed by the investment of the Duke of Norfolk, who named his 'industrial quarter' after the family name, Howard Town. The heyday of the already ancient lead mining industry was in the 18th and 19th centuries. The best-preserved remains are at Magpie Mine, near Sheldon, which was worked for over two centuries. Copper was mined at Ecton Hill above the Manifold Valley in Staffordshire by the Dukes of Devonshire, and it is said that the 5th Duke was able to build the classical Crescent at Buxton from the wealth won from Ecton Hill copper.

Macclesfield Silk Mill Museum

The building in 1830 of the Cromford and High Peak Railway, linking the Cromford Canal with the Peak Forest Canal at Whaley Bridge, marked the start of the railway age. It was followed by the Midland line through the Wye valley between Matlock and Buxton in 1860 and later by the unsuccessful Ashbourne to Buxton line that crossed the White Peak plateau. Later, some of the same navvies living in temporary villages were to build the mighty reservoirs in Longdendale and the Upper Derwent Valley, built like all the Peak District's 50 reservoirs to slake the insatiable thirst of the surrounding cities.

Rudyard Reservoir

Bakewell Carnival

Folklore and Festivals

Buxton well dressing

Garland King and Queen

There is a strong tradition of non-conformism in the Peak District, reflected in the Methodist chapels that still exist in most villages and towns.

But the Christian religion failed to extinguish all the ancient traditions that stem from pagan times, and many are still celebrated in the area. Chief among these is the unique custom of well dressing, thought to be a customary pagan thanksgiving for the gift of spring water on the high and usually dry limestone plateau.

About 20 villages still celebrate this custom, in which a design, usually biblical, is pricked out on clay pressed into panels and then coloured in by the use of flower petals and naturally-found materials. The result is erected over the village well or spring, usually the night before the village Wakes Week, in celebration of the patron saint of the local church. Next morning, often coinciding with the village carnival or fete, the well dressing is blessed by the local priest. The dressing stands for about a week, attracting the admiration of thousands of visitors.

The Castleton Garlanding is another very ancient ceremony, thought to be a celebration of the return of spring. It takes place on 29 May, Oak Apple Day, when a 'King' and 'Queen' dressed in Jacobean clothes tour the village on horseback. The King is completely encased in the garland, a heavy bell-shaped framework covered in wild flowers, which is eventually hoisted to the top of the village church at the end of the day.

A rushbearing ceremony still takes place at the remote Macclesfield Forest Chapel, and a Methodist 'Love Feast', recalling the times when worshippers had to meet in secret, happens every July in a barn at Alport Castles Farm, just off the Snake Road in the shadow of Bleaklow.

Calendar of events

Actual dates of events such as well dressings and agricultural shows vary slightly from year to year, so the following is only a rough guide. For precise dates get a copy of the Peak National Park free newspaper, *Peakland Post*, which has authoritative listings of events, or check with the local tourist information centre.

The fine art of well dressing

February/March
Winster Pancake Race (Shrove Tuesday); Ashbourne Shrovetide Football (Shrove Tuesday/Ash Wednesday).

May
Tissington Well Dressing (Ascension Day); Bamford Sheepdog Trials; Chatsworth Angling Fair; Leek Arts Festival; Wirksworth Well Dressing and Carnival; Monyash Well Dressing; Middleton-by-Youlgreave Well Dressing; Ashford in the Water Well Dressing; Castleton Garland Ceremony (Oak Apple Day, May 29).

June
Chelmorton Flower Festival; Youlgreave Well Dressing; Litton Well Dressing; Tideswell Well Dressing; Hope Well Dressing; Bakewell Well Dressing and Carnival; Rowsley Well Dressing; Harden Moss Sheepdog Trials.

65

Fun and games in Bakewell

July
Leek Show; Glossop Carnival; Baslow Well Dressing; Bamford Well Dressing; Longstones Well Dressing; Stoney Middleton Well Dressing; Buxton Well Dressing; Buxton International Festival of Opera and Art; Alport Love Feast; Chesterfield Medieval Market.

August
Bakewell Agricultural Show (first week); Hope Sheepdog Trials and Agricultural Show; Chatsworth Country Fair; Matlock Carnival; Dove Dale Sheepdog Trials; Ashbourne Show; Macclesfield Fun Day; Bradwell Well Dressing; Great Hucklow Well Dressing; Taddington Well Dressing; Eyam Well Dressing; Foolow Well Dressing.

The band plays on

September
Longshaw Sheepdog Trials; Chatsworth International Sheepdog Trials; Hayfield Sheepdog Trials; Wirksworth Festival of Music; Longnor Races; Penistone Agricultural Show; Wardlow Well Dressing.

November/December
Castleton Christmas Lights; Ashbourne Christmas Lights and Entertainment; Raft Race at Matlock and Matlock Bath (Boxing Day); Dove Dale Dash.

THE OLD ORIGINAL

· BAKEWELL ·

PUDDING SHOP

LICENSED
RESTAURANT

AIR COND

Food and Drink

Opposite: a tempting sign

The most famous delicacy to come from the Peak District is probably the Bakewell tart. But visitors should never call it a tart in the ancient town of its birthplace by the River Wye. Here it is always known as the Bakewell pudding, and various shops in the town produce their own versions following jealously guarded secret recipes. The story goes that a harassed cook at the Rutland Arms in the centre of the town produced the dish by accident, after putting the pastry on top of the jam, instead of the other way round. It was a great hit with the diners and is now exported all around the world, looking and tasting nothing like the commercial 'tart'.

Bakewell puddings

Ashbourne, the pleasant market town on the southern edge of the Peak, prides itself on its own special brand of gingerbread, usually made in the shape of the gingerbread man of the fairy story. Much of the milk from Peak District farms comes to the large Ashbourne factory that produces Nestlé's chocolate and other products. Other milk is taken by tankers to Hartington where another large factory produces 'the King of English Cheeses' – Stilton. Hartington only just qualifies for this honour, because it can only be produced in the counties of Nottinghamshire, Leicestershire or Derbyshire – and the boundary with Staffordshire is only half a mile away. The highly-flavoured, crumbly blue cheese is matured in large stores and, like the pudding, exported around the world.

Gingerbread men

A more recent introduction to the specialist foods of the Peak District has been commercial mineral water. The health-giving qualities of Buxton's waters have, of course, been long known, but they have more recently been joined by Wildboarclough water, collected from hillside springs on the Cheshire side of the Peak.

Restaurant selection

The following restaurants are selected from some of the region's most popular destinations and listed according to two categories: £££ = expensive; ££ = moderate.

Fine dining

Ashbourne

Callow Hall Country House and Restaurant, Mappleton Road, tel: 01335 343403. Set in glorious wooded grounds half a mile from the centre of Ashbourne, this elegant Victorian house provides high-class English and Continental cuisine. £££.

Ashford in the Water

Riverside Country House Hotel, tel: 01629 814275. In a beautiful position overlooking the River Wye, the gourmet restaurant in the conservatory offers high-class cuisine in a lovely setting. £££. **The Ashford Hotel and Restaurant**, Church Street, tel: 01629 812725. Offers full table d'hôte and à la carte selections, plus Sunday lunches and bar meals. ££.

Restaurants traditional…

Bakewell

Rutland Arms Hotel, Rutland Square, tel: 01629 812812. 'Home' of the Bakewell Pudding and allegedly featured in *Pride and Prejudice* (Jane Austen stayed here), the Rutland Arms is Bakewell's most famous restaurant. ££. **Milford House Hotel**, Mill Street, tel: 01629 812130. Traditional English cooking in a quiet and homely family-run setting. ££.

…and modern

Buxton

Lee Wood Hotel, The Park, Buxton, tel: 01298 23002. The award-winning Garden Room Restaurant specialises in pre- and post-theatre meals for visitors to the nearby Opera House. Evening brasserie. ££.

Dove Dale

Izaak Walton Hotel, Thorpe, tel: 01335 350555. The dining room, overlooking Dove Dale, is Regency style and specialises in English and French dishes. ££.

Booking essential

Hassop

Hassop Hall Hotel, Hassop, tel: 01629 640488. This is one of the finest hotels and restaurants in the Peak District, and booking for meals is essential. The menu is extensive and the quality unmatched. £££.

Hathersage

The George Hotel, Main Road, Hathersage, tel: 01433 650436. The Charlotte Restaurant serves a combination of traditional and Continental dishes, while the George Bar offers delicious home-made pies. ££.

Hope

The Poacher's Arms, Castleton Road, Hope, tel: 01433 620380. On the outskirts of Hope, specialities include homemade poacher's soup. ££.

Matlock

Riber Hall Hotel, Riber, tel: 01629 582475. A fine Tudor hotel and restaurant in a beautiful setting. Outstanding French and English cuisine for the connoisseur. £££.

Rowsley

Peacock Hotel, Rowsley, tel: 01629 733518. Favoured by anglers fishing the River Wye, the Peacock also has a fine restaurant offering a lunchtime buffet. ££.

Active Holidays

Decision time

Walking

Walking is easily the most popular outdoor pursuit in the Peak District. Whatever the weather, there will always be people on the 1,600 miles (2,600km) of public rights of way. Some of the toughest walks in Britain cross the high, featureless Dark Peak moors of Kinder Scout, Bleaklow and Black Hill. At the other extreme, gentle paths follow crystal rivers in White Peak dales. One of the Peak's greatest pleasures is a riverside stroll through abundant trees in a limestone dale. Walking the limestone plateau is another delight, where way-marked paths lead from village to village and ancient trackways link Bronze Age hilltop burial mounds or lows.

Although the broad, bleak plateaus of the Dark Peak only just top the 2,000-ft (610-m) mark, they are often underestimated by visiting walkers. The combination of featureless bogs, deep winding 'groughs' (natural drainage channels) and soft, slippery 'hags' (banks of peat) make navigation a real challenge. Aficionados who relish such challenges are known as bogtrotters.

Until the 1930s, most of the high and wild moors were barred to walkers and kept sacrosanct for the grouse raised to be shot after the 'Glorious Twelfth' of August. But one April Sunday in 1932, a well-publicised 'mass trespass' took place on Kinder Scout. Five ramblers were imprisoned for riotous behaviour. The 'Battle for Kinder Scout' sparked the National Parks and Access to the Countryside movement.

Taking it all in from Stanage

The Peak National Park was created in 1951 and agreements with major moorland landowners followed. There is now open access to over 80sq miles (207sq km) of the Dark Peak moors, subject to commonsense by-laws and short closures for shooting. Tom Stephenson's Pennine

Way was designed to open up the forbidden Peak District moors. It starts from Edale (*see page 43*).

Dove Dale is the most famous White Peak dale, and it is very busy at the height of summer. Monsal Dale, Lathkill Dale, Bradford Dale and the Manifold Valley are also popular. There is easy walking on the former railway tracks of the Tissington, High Peak, Monsal and Manifold Trails, and the Longdendale Trail in the far north. The Limestone Way is a pleasant waymarked north-south route through the White Peak between Matlock and Castleton.

Climbing

The Peak District can claim to be the birthplace of modern rock climbing. Certainly, it is the headquarters of the hard rock school, with thousands of routes snaking up the gritstone edges and limestone crags of the area.

Middle-class businessmen took to the gritstone crags early in the 20th century, but the real explosion started in the 1950s when two Manchester plumbers, Joe Brown and Don Whillans, took to crags such as Stanage Edge and The Roaches. In the years that followed, the Peak gave birth to a new generation of world-class climbers.

It is a measure of progress that routes once thought to be impossible on the crags of High Tor at Matlock, Stoney Middleton and Chee Tor are now climbed without ropes.

A new generation of climber

The Witch's Shadow, Treak Cliff Cavern

Caving

Although Peak District limestone lacks the huge gaping potholes of the Yorkshire Dales (only Eldon Hole, near Peak Forest, comes into this category), there are many miles of sporting caves, especially in the Castleton area. Giant's Hole, near Sparrowpit, is one of the longest and deepest routes in Britain, with challenging obstacles like the narrow Crab Walk, while others like Oxlow Caverns and Nettle Pot demand equal skill and experience.

Tourists are advised to inspect the underground wonders of the Peak in the public showcaves of Castleton (Treak Cliff, Blue John, Speedwell and Peak Cavern, the largest cave entrance in Britain), Bagshawe Cavern at Bradwell (which runs adventure trips), Poole's Cavern at Buxton, and Matlock's Great Rutland Cavern.

Cycling in the Goyt Valley

Cycling

Walkers on the Tissington and High Peak Trails and the Manifold Track, former railway routes in the White Peak, share their path with an increasing number of cyclists, many of whom will have hired their machines from the cycle hire centres provided by the National Park authority at former stations. This is an ideal and very popular way to explore the White Peak countryside in traffic-free conditions that are perfect for children.

The growing army of mountain bikers are catered for with more challenging routes on bridleways. The hiring centre at Fairholmes in the Upper Derwent Valley is a convenient base to explore this wilder country. Published guides explain where mountain bikers can go.

Horse-riding

In control

Most of the Peak's bridleways were originally used by packhorse trains in medieval times, including Jacob's Ladder in western Edale and Doctor's Gate over Snake Pass.

Former railway lines such as the Tissington, High Peak and Monsal Trails across the White Peak plateau and the Manifold Valley Track in Staffordshire are also ideal for traffic-free riding. The latest is the Longdendale Trail, in the far north of the National Park, passing through the Woodhead Valley. This is part of the Trans-Pennine Trail that links Merseyside and Humberside.

There are stables around the Peak District, including Edale, where horses can be hired and training is given.

Nature watching

With research based in the universities of nearby cities and the long tradition of amateur naturalists like the Sorby Club in Sheffield and various bird study groups in Manchester, Peak District wildlife has been extensively studied.

Many limestone dales in the White Peak are protected as National Nature Reserves. They are the botanical highlights of the Peak District, with over 50 species of plants per sq metre. These include the beautiful yellow rockrose, a variety of orchids, and cushions of thyme and vetches that attract clouds of butterflies. The ash woods of Dove Dale and Lathkill Dale are of national importance. They support the rare purple-flowered shrub mezereon, and wood anemones and dog's mercury carpet the shaded woodland floor.

Birdwatchers wait for spring when the summer migrants appear, including golden plovers on the moors and pied flycatchers in the Derwent oakwoods. Around the reservoirs of the Upper Derwent is an internationally important population of goshawk. These reservoirs also offer the closest thing to wetlands in the Peak, and they see rare waders like the common sandpiper. Golden plovers and curlews haunt the moors, and a few black grouse hang on in Staffordshire: their 'leks' are kept secret.

The rarest Peak mammals include Britain's southernmost colony of blue or mountain hares on the eastern moors. They were reintroduced for sport at the turn of the century, and their coats go white in winter. More common mammals are well represented, the largest being the herds of red deer in the parklands of Chatsworth and Lyme Park near Stockport.

71

Limestone country: the Derwent Gorge

Close to nature at the Heights of Abraham

Getting There

By car

One reason the Peak District receives so many visitors is its accessibility. Surrounded by the conurbations of the North and the Midlands, more than 100 roads run into and through the National Park. It is also the nearest National Park to London and the southeast, easily reached by the M1 motorway – junctions 28 (Matlock) for the White Peak and southern dales and 29 (Chesterfield) for the central and northern areas. Motorists coming from the west should leave the M6 at junction 18 (Congleton) or 19 (Knutsford). A pleasant introduction to the varied landscapes of the Peak District is to use the A6 trunk road, which winds through the valley of the River Wye from Matlock via Bakewell to Buxton.

Heading through Matlock

By coach

National Express daily coach services link the Peak District with London and Manchester. The 350 and 351 from Liverpool, Manchester, Sheffield and East Anglia call at Crowden, Langsett, Sheffield and Chesterfield. The 440 connects Buxton, Macclesfield, Derby, Leicester and London: it runs through the heart of the Peak District, calling at Ashbourne, Buxton, Bakewell, Matlock and Matlock Bath. For more information, tel: 0990 808080.

By train

Midland and East Coast InterCity express trains provide a regular service of around two hours from London St Pancras to Derby, Chesterfield and Sheffield. The West Coast route to Stoke and Manchester starts from London Euston, and again there are regular services. The InterCity Cross-Country route between Newcastle and Plymouth passes through Derby, Chesterfield and Sheffield. For further information, tel: 0800 125222, 01332 257000, 0161 832 8353 or 0114 253 7676.

Local services link Derby and Nottingham with Matlock; Stockport with Buxton and Glossop; and Birmingham and Stoke-on-Trent with Macclesfield. The Peak also has a local service running through its centre. The Hope Valley line, run by Regional Rail and still known as the Ramblers' Route, links Sheffield and Stockport via Grindleford, Hathersage, Bamford, Hope and Edale.

Buxton station

By air

Manchester Airport at Ringway is the nearest airport to the Peak District, and it is served by intercontinental as well as internal flights. Manchester Airport is just off the M56, south of Manchester near Wilmslow. For flight information, tel: 0161 489 3000.

Getting Around

Few National Parks are as well served with public transport, both bus and train, as the Peak District. The Peak District Bus and Train Timetable, published by Derbyshire County Council, is updated annually and is essential reading for visitors without a car. The Derbyshire Wayfarer ticket enables visitors to enjoy one day's unlimited travel on all buses and trains in the county, including services to or from Sheffield, Macclesfield, Leek, Uttoxeter and Burton-on-Trent. Tickets are obtainable from most bus-travel and tourist-information offices.

Buses

The Peak District Bus and Rail Timetable, mentioned above, is the key to using buses to explore the area. Many local bus companies also run scenic tours during the summer season. Check locally for details.

Trains

As mentioned on page 73, the Hope Valley line is an excellent way to explore the Hope and Edale Valleys in the north of the Peak. Regular services run between Sheffield and Stockport, calling at Grindleford, Hathersage, Bamford, Hope, Edale, Chinley and Whaley Bridge. These are convenient for linear walks between stations, and some services will carry bicycles free of charge. Other services link Manchester and Stockport with Buxton, Glossop and Macclesfield. For information, tel: 0161 832 8353.

Up hill and down dale

Taxis and car rental

There are taxi ranks in Sheffield, Chesterfield, Matlock, Buxton, Glossop, Leek, Ashbourne and Macclesfield. Within the Peak, there is no shortage of taxi and car hire services. Check locally for details.

Cycle hire

Parsley Hay cycle hire centre

The former railway lines of the Longdendale, Tissington and High Peak, Monsal and Manifold Trails are perfect for family cycling, with no traffic, sharp bends or big hills to negotiate. Traffic-free roads ideal for cycling can also be found in the Upper Derwent Valley when the road closure scheme is operating at weekends and Bank Holidays. Cycle hire centres, with reduced rates between September and March, are situated at: Ashbourne Tissington Trail, tel: 01335 343156; Parsley Hay Tissington Trail, tel: 01298 84493; Waterhouses Manifold Track, tel: 01538 308609; Fairholmes Upper Derwent, tel: 01433 651261; Middleton Top High Peak Trail, tel: 01629 823204; Hayfield Sett Valley Trail, tel: 01663 746222; Shipley Country Park, near Heanor, tel: 01773 719961.

Facts for the Visitor

Tourist and visitor information

There are many information centres around the Peak. Those marked * will book accommodation. Ask for a copy of *Peakland Post*, the Park's free annual newspaper, for a full list of events and places. ***Ashbourne**, Market Place, tel: 01335 300638; ***Bakewell**, Old Market Hall, tel: 01629 813227; ***Buxton**, The Crescent, tel: 01298 25106; **Castleton**, Castle Street, tel: 01433 620679; ***Chesterfield**, Peacock Centre, tel: 01246 207777/8; **Edale**, Fieldhead, tel: 01433 670207; **Fairholmes**, Upper Derwent, tel: 01433 650953; ***Glossop**, Victoria Street, tel: 01457 855920; **Hartington Signal Box**, on the Tissington Trail; ***Holmfirth**, Huddersfield Road, tel: 01484 687603; **Langsett**, near Stocksbridge; ***Leek**, Market Place, tel: 01538 381000; ***Macclesfield**, Town Hall, tel: 01625 504112; ***Matlock Bath**, The Pavilion, tel: 01629 55082; **Torside**, Longdendale.

Outside Bakewell Tourist Information Centre

Emergencies

To call for emergency police, fire or medical assistance dial 999 from any telephone. The following accident and casualty departments are open 24 hours every day. **Major casualties**: Stockport Infirmary, Wellington Road South, tel: 0161 483 1010; Derby Royal Infirmary, London Road, tel: 01332 347141; Chesterfield Royal Hospital, Calow, tel: 01246 277271. **Major child casualties**: Children's Hospital, Western Bank, Sheffield, tel: 0114 2761111. **Minor casualties**: Buxton Cottage Hospital, London Road, tel: 01298 22293; Whitworth Hospital, Bakewell Road, tel: 01629 584754; St Oswald's Hospital, Belle View Road, Ashbourne, tel: 01335 342121.

Facilities for disabled people

A wheelchair-accessible path runs through lower Dove Dale, and there are trails for disabled people at Fairholmes, Upper Derwent Valley, and Dovestone Reservoir. The railway trails – Tissington, High Peak, Manifold, Monsal and Longdendale – are accessible to disabled people, and special cycles at the Fairholmes and Parsley Hay hire centres let those in wheelchairs ride the trails.

Market days and early closing

Ashbourne: early closing Wednesday; market Saturday. **Bakewell**: early closing Thursday; market on Monday. **Buxton**: early closing Wednesday; markets Saturday (main) and Tuesday (small). **Castleton**: early closing Wednesday. **Glossop**: early closing Tuesday; markets Friday and Saturday outdoor, Thursday indoor. **Matlock**: early closing Thursday; markets Tuesday and Friday.

Glossop Open Air Market

Starting young on Stanage

Castleton: young participants at the Garland Ceremony

Adventure at Chatsworth

Fun at Matlock

The Peak District for Children

John Ruskin described Derbyshire as 'a lovely child's alphabet; an alluring first lesson in all that is admirable...' Generations of school parties have endorsed that testimonial, and places like Castleton are still popular for school visits from surrounding towns and cities.

A special education and day-visit service is run from the National Park Study Centre at Losehill Hall, Castleton, tel: 01433 620373. The Ranger Service runs a programme of children's fun days and activities throughout the summer. For details, tel: 01629 815185.

Special attractions for children include the **Children's Farmyard and Adventure Playground**, Chatsworth (mid-March to end of September 10.30am–4.30/5pm, playground only October weekends and half-term noon–4.30pm); the **National Stone Centre**, Wirksworth (October to March daily 10am–4pm, March to October, 10am–5pm, closed Christmas Day and Boxing Day); the **Blackbrook World of Birds and Animals**, Winkhill near Leek (April to October daily 11.30am–5.30pm, November to March weekends only); the **National Tramway Museum**, Crich (April to October daily 10am–5pm, March and November Sunday only), and **Gulliver's Kingdom Family Theme Park**, Matlock Bath (Easter to late September daily 10.30am–5pm, late September to end October, weekends only).

Alton Towers (March to November, park from 9am, rides from 10am, closes 6–6.30pm, tel: 0990 204060) is 18 miles (30km) southwest of Ashbourne via the A52 and B5032. The 200-acre (80-hectare) parkland features big rides and Storybook Land for younger visitors. There are firework displays in autumn from 6–6.30pm.

Accommodation

As a general rule, hotels lie outside the central area of the park, inside it is mainly bed and breakfast. Annual accommodation guides are produced by the East Midlands Tourist Board, tel: 01522 531521, the Derbyshire Dales District Council, tel: 01629 580580, and the Peak District National Park, tel: 01629 816200. The guides are also available from information centres together with a comprehensive annual Caravan and Camping Site Guide, including details for booking ahead.

The Park also runs 13 Camping Barns, which offer very basic 'stone tent' sleeping accommodation in converted barns for just £3 a night. For more details and to book, tel: 01433 620373.

Hartington Hall
Youth Hostel

Below are some larger hotels, costing per night for a double room approximately: **£££** = over £80; **££** = over £50; **£** = up to £50.

Ashbourne

Ashbourne Lodge Hotel, Derby Road, tel: 01335 702265. Modern, large, comfortable hotel with new leisure centre. Convenient for Dove Dale and Alton Towers. ££. **Bentley Brook Inn**, Fenny Bentley, A515 Buxton Road just north of Ashbourne, tel: 01335 350278. Large country-house inn very close to Dove Dale and convenient for the whole of the White Peak. ££.

Ashford in the Water

Ashford Hotel & Restaurant, Church Street, tel: 01629 812725. Traditional country-house hotel and restaurant by the River Wye and a sheepwash bridge. £££. **Riverside Country House Hotel**, tel: 01629 814275. Small 18th-century country house on the Wye. Four-poster beds, log fires and antiques. £££.

Riverside Country House Hotel

Bakewell

Milford House Hotel, Mill Street, tel: 01629 812130. Peaceful Georgian hotel in its own grounds; family-run with traditional English cooking. ££.

Milford House Hotel

Buxton

Buckingham Hotel, Burlington Road, tel: 01298 70481. Three-star hotel with excellent cuisine overlooking the Pavilion Gardens. ££. **Grosvenor House Hotel**, Broad Walk, tel: 01298 72439. Views extend across the Pavilion Gardens to the Edwardian Opera House. ££. **Lee Wood Hotel**, The Park, tel: 01298 23002. Elegant, three-star Georgian hotel in its own grounds close to the centre of town; award-winning Garden Room Restaurant. ££.

Buxton: Old Hall Hotel

Old Hall Hotel, The Square, tel: 01298 22841. Historic hotel opposite the Pavilion Gardens; Mary Queen of Scots was a 'guest' in 1576–8. ££. **Palace Hotel**, Palace Road, tel: 01298 22001. Buxton's premier hotel, recently renovated; features Dove Dale Restaurant and Oasis Leisure Centre. ££. **Buxton Wheelhouse Hotel**, College Road, tel: 01298 24869. Elegant Victorian hotel by the Grinlow Country Park and Poole's Cavern; personal service and excellent home cooking. £. **Hartington Hotel**, Broad Walk, tel: 01298 22638. Overlooks the Pavilion Gardens in the town centre; family run for nearly 40 years. £. **Portland Hotel & Restaurant**, St. John's Road, tel: 01298 71493. Award-winning restaurant in the elegant conservatory; family-run hotel. ££. **Staden Grange Hotel**, Staden Lane, off the A515 Ashbourne road, tel: 01298 24965. In open farmland; claims the warmest welcome in Derbyshire; offers aromatherapy, reflexology and therapeutic massage. £.

Castleton

Kelsey's Swiss House, How Lane, tel: 01433 621098. Small country house hotel. £. **Ye Olde Nags Head Hotel**, Castleton, tel: 01433 620248. Former 17th-century coaching house in the centre of the village. ££.

Dove Dale

Izaak Walton Hotel, Dove Dale, tel: 01335 350555. One of the Peak's most stylish and famous hotels, in the jaws of Dove Dale beneath Thorpe Cloud. £££.

Glossop Golf Course

Glossop

The Wind in the Willows, Derbyshire Level, off the Snake Road (A57), tel: 01457 868001. Views to Bleaklow; former Best Small Hotel in North of England. ££.

Great Longstone

Croft Country House Hotel, Great Longstone, tel: 01629 640278. Recently tastefully converted; Victorian country house in its own grounds. £££.

Hartington

Charles Cotton Hotel, Market Place, tel: 01298 84229. Cosy hotel; good food and real ale. £. **Manifold Valley Hotel**, Hulme End, tel: 01298 84537. On the banks of the River Manifold, which disappears in the summer. £.

Hassop

Hassop Hall Hotel, tel: 01629 640488. One of the Peak's most elegant venues; classical Georgian house formerly owned by the Eyre family; in spacious parkland 2 miles (3km) from Bakewell. £££.

Hathersage

George Hotel, Main Road, tel: 01433 650436. Former 16th-century coaching inn; lovely garden and a fine restaurant. ££. **Millstone Inn**, Sheffield Road, tel: 01433 650258. Recently refurbished; above the village with fine views down the Hope Valley to Kinder Scout. ££.

Hope

Woodroffe Arms Hotel, Castleton Road, tel: 01433 620351. Traditional Peak country inn; 1 mile (1.5km) from Castleton and 4 miles (6.5km) from Edale. £.

George Hotel

Matlock

Riber Hall Hotel, Matlock, tel: 01629 582475. Nominated one of the most romantic hotels in Britain; Tudor mansion high above the town; wonderful views from ancient, mullioned windows. £££. **Dales and Peaks Hotel**, Old Road, Darley Dale, on the A6 north of Matlock, tel: 01629 733775. Elegant Victorian country house renowned for Victorian Supper Evenings. ££. **Jackson Tor House Hotel**, Jackson Road, tel: 01629 582348. Family-run hotel overlooking Matlock and surrounds; traditional English breakfasts. £. **Old English Hotel**, Dale Road, tel: 01629 55028. Recently refurbished Victorian Gothic hotel; central with a warm, family-run atmosphere. £.

79

Matlock Bath

New Bath Hotel, New Bath Road, on the A6 between Matlock Bath and Cromford, tel: 01629 583275. Large Victorian hotel overlooking the gorge of the River Derwent; swimming pool, solarium, tennis courts and play area. £££. **Temple Hotel**, Temple Walk, tel: 01629 583911. In a commanding position overlooking Matlock Bath and the Derwent Gorge; specialises in Austrian food. ££.

Monsal Dale

Castle Cliffe Hotel, Monsal Head, tel: 01629 640258. Victorian stone house overlooking one of the most famous views in the Peak District at Monsal Head; log fires and traditional home-made food. £.

The Peacock, near Chatsworth

Rowsley

Rowsley is convenient for Chatsworth and Haddon. **East Lodge Country House Hotel**, just off the A6, tel: 01629 734474. Charming and tastefully furnished country house in 10 acres (12 hectares) of its own grounds; the restaurant has a good reputation. ££. **Peacock Hotel**, tel: 01629 733518. Fine old listed hotel named after the peacock emblem of the Manners family which stands guard over the entrance; famous in the world of angling for fine fishing in the nearby River Wye. £££.

Index